Praise for *In the Common Interest II*

"Like Associa, Brookfield Residential has built a reputation as an industry leader and innovator. Our focus on continuously aspiring to improve our delivery from our building practices to customer experience is part of our culture. *In the Common Interest II: Delivering Five Star Customer Service* echoes our commitment to always "do the right thing" for those we serve. Mr. Carona's humble approach recognizes that the customer experience is a journey, which is critical to building strong communities. His views are timely and will be impactful, especially in these days of rapid change and disruption."

—ADRIAN FOLEY, president & COO, Brookfield Residential

"As an HOA board member and state senator, I know firsthand the importance and challenges of providing excellent customer service with Aloha. With his new book, John Carona continues to demonstrate his role as a thoughtful leader in the community management industry. *In The Common Interest: Embracing Five Star Customer Service* provides a much-needed dialogue on service delivery in a fast-paced, ever-changing industry."

—MICHELLE KIDANI, HOA board member, Hawaii state senator

"Associa is a leader in the community association industry. As our industry is rooted in relationships and often misrepresented in the media, focusing on serving customers well during a period of industry transformation is a timely and needed topic."

—GREG SMITH, 2017 president, Community Associations Institute

"I have spent my entire career fixing things not done properly or poorly maintained. This book provides an inspiring approach to community living and civic pride that could transform how we interact within our micro and macro societies. A recommended read for everyone."

—MIKE HOLMES, TV host and Trusted Contractor

"John Carona, CEO of Associa, has done it again with the book *In the Common Interest II: Embracing Five Star Customer Service*. Mr. Carona debunks the myth that in 2018 all services and industries are commodities with no distinction among them. What's interesting is that so many things that Associa does have zero cost. It is all about empowerment. Meeting or exceeding expectations is obtainable once that type of culture is instilled in people, as Associa aspires to do. No matter what industry you are involved with, this book delves deeply into what changes a company from being good to being great. This book is a must-read and a game-changer."

—STEPHEN MARCUS, partner at Marcus, Errico, Emmer & Brooks, past president of the CAI, College of Community Association Lawyers, recipient of the CAI Don Buck Lifetime Achievement Award

Embracing Five Star
Customer Service

IN THE
COMMON
INTEREST
2

JOHN CARONA

GREENLEAF
BOOK GROUP PRESS

Published by Greenleaf Book Group Press
Austin, Texas
www.gbgpress.com

Distributed by Greenleaf Book Group

For ordering information or special discounts for bulk purchases, please contact Greenleaf Book Group at PO Box 91869, Austin, TX 78709, 512.891.6100.

Design and composition by Greenleaf Book Group
Cover design by Greenleaf Book Group

Publisher's Cataloging-in-Publication data is available.

Print ISBN: 978-1-62634-462-4

eBook ISBN: 978-1-62634-463-1

Part of the Tree Neutral® program, which offsets the number of trees consumed in the production and printing of this book by taking proactive steps, such as planting trees in direct proportion to the number of trees used: www.treeneutral.com

TreeNeutral

Printed in the United States of America on acid-free paper

18 19 20 21 22 23 24   10 9 8 7 6 5 4 3 2 1

First Edition

To those innovators from throughout Associa who possess the vision and the courage to reshape our industry.

CONTENTS

INTRODUCTION   1

PART I:
OUR FOUNDATION   7

CHAPTER 1:
Our Story   11

CHAPTER 2:
Our Clients and Customers   21

CHAPTER 3:
Our Service Model   29

PART II:
OUR SERVICE CULTURE   33

CHAPTER 4:
Our Mission and Pillars   37

CHAPTER 5:
Our Values at Work   45

CHAPTER 6:
Our Five Star Customer Service Model   53

PART III:
DELIVERING OUR SERVICE INTERNALLY   65

CHAPTER 7:
Demonstrating How We Serve Each Other   69

CHAPTER 8:
Internalizing Our Five Star Customer Service Model   75

CHAPTER 9:
Serving while Leading   81

CHAPTER 10:
Selecting and Educating the Right People   89

CHAPTER 11:
Communicating with Our Teams   97

CHAPTER 12:
Retaining Our People   105

CHAPTER 13:
Rewarding Service Heroes   113

PART IV:
DELIVERING OUR SERVICE EXTERNALLY   121

CHAPTER 14:
Demonstrating Care   125

CHAPTER 15:
Communicating with Customers   135

CHAPTER 16:
Leading within Our Communities   151

CHAPTER 17:
Building Relationships   159

CHAPTER 18:
Owning the Resolution   171

CHAPTER 19:
Giving Back to Our Community at Large   177

PART V:
DEALING WITH SHORTCOMINGS IN SERVICE   183

CHAPTER 20:
Stepping toward Customer Service Recovery   187

CHAPTER 21:
Recovering from Service Failures   199

CHAPTER 22:
Serving through Change   207

PART VI:
OUR WAY FORWARD   215

CHAPTER 23:
Measuring Our Momentum   219

CHAPTER 24:
Continuing to Lead the Way   227

CONCLUSION   237

ACKNOWLEDGMENTS   243

INDEX   245

ABOUT THE AUTHOR   253

INTRODUCTION

*Service, in short, is not what you do, but who you are. It is
a way of living that you bring to everything you do,
if you are to bring it to your customers.*

—BETSY SANDERS,
Author and Former Nordstrom Executive

No company can be successful without a passionate dedication to customer service. Whether we describe it as exemplary, excellent, outstanding, unsurpassed, or five star customer service, our goal must be to provide the best service we can. Only by striving to exceed our customers' needs and expectations can we develop the loyalty needed for a long and lasting brand. These realizations are the bedrock of my forty-year career in community association management and underscore my perspective and experience, especially as chairman and chief executive officer of Associa.

I learned the importance of customer service at an early age. Some say Associa began when I earned my first lawn-mowing job when I was twelve, a job that grew quickly to serving twenty homeowners a week. It planted the seed for my growing interest in the service industry.

Growing up a child of Italian heritage, however, it was my father who showed me that serving others meant going above and beyond.

In the grocery store he owned in the small town of Dickinson, Texas, there wasn't a job he didn't do or wasn't willing to do. What's more, he expected the same of his employees and relatives, many of whom worked alongside him daily. Little did I know then that the lessons I observed as a child would become the principles upon which I would build my own company one day.

Similarly, there isn't a job at Associa that I haven't done, regardless of how menial it may seem, and I expect the same of any leader in our organization. We simply do what needs to be done, and nothing should be too big or too small for us if it is important to our customers. If it matters to them, it should matter to us—period.

Our clients trust us to help them protect the value of their most precious assets—their homes and the communities in which they live. In doing so, we develop unique relationships with community association boards, homeowners, and vendors while offering a rich variety of services designed to protect and enhance their property values. This requires us to be flexible and to perform in multiple ways, ranging from showing leadership in solving complex problems to serving our clients' smallest needs. It also requires us to transition quickly and seamlessly from working with our clients, namely, community association boards of directors, to working on their behalf to provide services for their customers and ours, namely, homeowners.

Associa's best practices for five star service are not unique to our company or to business in general. Frankly, the best practices for internal and external customer service revolve around treating others well. Being nice, likable, and trustworthy are good habits to practice at work, at home, or in the community.

WHY THIS BOOK?

My first book, *In the Common Interest: Embracing the New American Community*, examined the foundations of the community management industry. I see that as the "what" of our business. This sequel, *In the Common Interest II: Embracing Five Star Customer Service*, is its "how." My purpose herein includes defining and describing Associa's Five Star Customer Service Model, which captures my belief that building a business by successfully practicing the principles of community management depends on a foundation of providing excellent customer service. The outlook for a company that does otherwise ultimately is failure.

Through this book I hope to share with every Associa employee and customer our deeply held core value of customer service and how we strive to deliver on that commitment every day in every way. This includes little things like not leaving for the day until we've responded to our customers and to each other—returning phone calls, responding to emails, or following up to ensure action items were accomplished. It also includes big things like responding in the middle of the night to an unexpected disaster. Most important, it requires our deliberate and focused attention to providing the best possible customer service while serving those we are privileged to call our employees and our clients.

Most of the examples and stories I share are small everyday acts of service that touch our employees' and clients' lives and impact their communities. It is my intent through these pages to present a path to great service for those within our industry and those outside it while giving you, the reader, key takeaways that you can begin to use immediately, regardless of the job you do or the industry in which you work.

ISSUES AND CHAPTERS

Because we are not your typical business, this is not your typical customer service book. Its twenty-four chapters are organized into six parts that capture our performance and aspirations.

While the intent to deliver excellent or five star customer service should be common to all service businesses, the way in which we at Associa must perform our duty often is defined by our contractual obligations. These obligations are discussed in Part I, Our Foundation, which also defines more fully Associa's service model as well as the nature of our relationships with our clients and customers.

Part II, Our Service Culture, expands on the foundation on which our service is built, namely, our mission, pillars, and values. This foundation has served us well throughout the decades and will continue to do so as we move into the future. It also introduces Associa's Five Star Customer Service Model, which is the focus of two parts of this book.

Part III, Delivering Our Service Internally, details how we live our philosophy internally by serving each other, including through effective leadership, communication, hiring and retention practices, and rewarding excellence. It demonstrates another of my strong beliefs: that just as charity begins at home, so does great customer service. Dependent on it, Part IV, Delivering Our Service Externally, provides examples of how our employees live this excellent service externally every day with our clients and customers and within the communities beyond the associations we manage.

Because nobody is perfect, and neither is Associa, Part V, Dealing with Shortcomings in Service, highlights how we handle situations when service goes wrong and when change requires special attention. It differentiates between issues resulting from misinformation or a lack of clear expectations and those caused by our making a mistake. Whatever the case, we prioritize our service recovery process.

Finally, Part VI, Our Way Forward, explains how we will evolve our Five Star Customer Service Model in a changing landscape. As technology and the market change, we must adapt our business model while remaining true to our foundation and to our service principles. Our mission, pillars, and values cumulatively compose our north star in the face of ever-changing industry standards and customer expectations. Our way forward will include measuring our progress as we prepare to continue to lead the way into our future as a company and as an industry leader.

As you read these chapters, I hope you will identify ways your industry and/or your role relates to what is entailed. Each ends with a "Service in Action" segment that highlights an Associa employee's success in meeting the needs of a client or customer. The questions at the end of each chapter will allow you to reflect and identify some action items that you can use to serve your customers and your industry better, whether they are the same or different from ours.

TERMINOLOGY

Our industry uses many words interchangeably, as illustrated herein. The terms "community association," "community," and "association" all are references to the entities that we manage. Other equally acceptable terms include "homeowners association" (or "HOA") and "planned unit development" (or "PUD"). For our friends and associates in Canada and across the globe, the common term for these entities is "stratas," and many times we refer to our employees in those locations as "strata managers."

Additionally, individual condominiums and homes in community associations often are referred to as "units," and their owners are called "homeowners" and "members." The latter refers to their membership in the association and differentiates them from renters who may live in the community but are not members.

We use "clients" to refer to the community associations and to the boards of directors or other entities who manage them and who hire us to assist them, even when they are referred to by other names. The term includes, for example, Canadian associations or communities and their boards, regardless of our reference to them as "strata" and as "councils," respectively.

We use "customers" to refer to their community association members, that is, to the homeowners who elect our board clients. These homeowners are the board's customers—and ours. Additionally, because most board members also are homeowners, they are both our clients and customers. To state it simply: Most clients (board members) are customers (homeowners), but not all customers (homeowners) are clients (board members). We use these terms accordingly. The exception, however, is that developers who serve as board members usually are not long-term homeowners or association members, but they often are our clients during the initial development of a new community association.

AUTHOR'S PERSPECTIVE

I want to be clear at the outset that we are not perfect. This book captures both what we do in our best moments and how we try to recover when we miss the mark. It is not my intent to be boastful or to imply that we get it right every time. As a service business, we are a people business, which means that mistakes will happen. As a learning organization, we are students of the process, which means that we will learn not only from what works well but also from what does not. In fact, some of the greatest service examples occur when we are attempting to recover from an original mistake.

What I am trying to illustrate is that our journey toward five star customer service is precisely that—a journey. I am grateful for our employees and for our clients who choose to join us along the way, and I hope this book illustrates how we welcome opportunities to lead this industry through serving both well. We will forever strive to make Associa a great place to work and a great partner with whom to work. We may not always be perfect, but we always try.

PART I

OUR

FOUNDATION

OUR FOUNDATION

We have entered the era of the customer. Today providing
customers with outstanding customer service is essential to
building loyal customers and a long-lasting brand.

—JERRY GREGOIRE,
Former CIO of Dell Computers

INTRODUCTION

We often use the metaphor of a house in our business, largely because
it is a concrete example that relates to the building of a structure and
the process of maintaining it. Just as a house with a weak foundation
eventually will fall, especially in the face of significant obstacles, so
will a business.

While many aspects of our industry and of our company have
changed over the years, one thing has remained the same: We built
Associa on a solid foundation of service that enables us to expand and
to withstand and overcome challenges. That effort also enables us to
build and to maintain loyal customers and a lasting brand.

Similarly, the three chapters that compose Part I will build a
foundation for this book by explaining more about who we are as a
company, differentiating our clients and customers, and defining our
service model. Cumulatively, they demonstrate how the elements
that make us different also can make providing excellent customer
service a challenge.

CHAPTER 1

Our Story

Customer Service represents the heart of
a brand in the hearts of its customers.

—KATE NASSER,
Executive Coach in Customer Service

In 1979 I started Associa with one client, less than $5,000, and big plans for the future. Community association management was fairly new and the market relatively small. Our industry was in its infancy, and my experience reflected my instincts and what I learned as I went along.

I believed then that homeowners who chose to live in a community association did so with higher expectations than most, and I wanted my company to be the industry leader on whom clients could depend for integrity, reliability, trustworthiness, and, above all, exceptional customer service. Since then we have grown to manage thousands of communities across the world. Both local and global, our service revolves around our customers as we focus on earning their loyalty while adapting to their needs and interests. The industry and Associa may have changed dramatically, but our passion for striving to be the best has never wavered.

Our company relies today on the same foundation upon which I established it. In the last four decades community management, along with almost everything else, has become a commodity. We can compete on price, but at the end of the day, it is our service level that will attract new clients and retain existing ones. From the beginning, our goal has been to build our company and our reputation by virtue of our loyalty, dependability, honesty, and unparalleled customer service.

OUR SCOPE

I never dreamed Associa would become what it is, but the foundation upon which we built it remains strong: service. Today I am proud to say we lead the industry. Associa is the largest and most stable management company in North America, and collectively, we manage more associations than any other company. Whether associations have ten homes or ten thousand, when we manage them, they can rest assured they are partnering with the industry leader in customer service, financial management, and information technology.

Through the years we have grown by winning new clients organically and by acquiring the best of the best management companies across the world and making them a part of our Associa family. Although our footprint is unmatched, we are keenly aware that with great success comes great responsibility. Regardless of our size, we can be vulnerable if we do not provide the best service and realize that service has changed dramatically since our early days. In evaluating our service, our customers do not merely compare us to our local community management competitor. They expect us to match or surpass the swift, personalized responses they get from their favorite fast or instant delivery or online company.

OUR PEOPLE

As a service business, our most important asset is our people. With forty years of experience and thousands of communities under our management, Associa has in-house expertise for every type of community association. We are the worldwide leader in managing homeowners associations, master-planned communities, high-rise condominiums, garden-style condos and townhomes, and office/commercial associations.

When we say that our people are our differentiator—what sets us apart from others—we mean we set high expectations beginning with how we treat one another, what we do for each other, and how we treat our customers. We search diligently to hire the most qualified candidates across our company to serve our homeowners associations. Our priority is to assemble leaders who have varied experience in our industry and beyond, including in financial services and hospitality. What we can learn from others makes us stronger as we continue to stay true to our roots and focus on our core of helping communities achieve their vision.

One of our common sayings is that we are better together than apart. That is true as we look internally to learn best practices from acquired companies and externally to other industries and different experiences. No matter how our industry changes, we always will be a people business. Our people, who work with our boards and home-owners every day, are who make us great. That is why we are so proud to have assembled the most talented and most accredited group of community managers in the industry. They are the ones who focus on providing excellent service to our customers daily.

OUR CONTINUING EDUCATION PROGRAMS

Our managers and all our employees have access to training and resources that cover every area of management, facilities maintenance, governance, and financial services. They are equipped with the information, skills, and educational programs they need to meet the complex range of demands that face the communities we serve. This includes being up to date on the latest best practices and all local, state, and federal regulations that may affect our clients; and maintaining community management licenses and certifications.

We make these resources available not only to our employees but also to board members and homeowners. We believe that the better educated our clients and customers are, the better our partnerships with them will be.

OUR VALUE TO OUR CLIENTS

The value of Associa is that we can put our size and strength to work for our clients. We have worked hard to achieve the industry's most rigorous financial standards and security measures, and we partner that expertise with many other values, including the best prices from trusted vendors, innovative technology, and the highest number of certified managers in the industry. What's more, we can scale our operations for any community, regardless of its size. We offer customized management solutions tailored to fit a client's specific needs, whatever they may be. By reinforcing our local expertise with our national resources, we enable our customers to live life better. Our core services are described below:

- Lifestyle Planning
- Community Governance
- Facilities Management
- Accounting and Financial Services
- Integrated Services

Lifestyle Planning

Our goal is to understand the vision our clients have for their communities and to partner with them to achieve it. Our expertise and experience with communities of all types and sizes allow us to provide consulting to help our board members and residents shape the communities of their dreams. Once that vision is established, we can deliver the resources to make that dream a reality—from architectural standards and project management to activities and engagement within the community.

Community Governance

Our teams are trained in the delicate balance of enforcing governing documents while maintaining a positive sense of community. We also specialize in streamlining the board's governance functions. Through our extensive knowledge and expertise, we assist our clients in coordinating and preparing for monthly and annual meetings. We also help them communicate and deal effectively in conflict management or dispute resolution among association members.

Facilities Management

Associa manages the administrative and operational needs of our clients' communities; assists with bidding, negotiating, and contracting aspects of dealing with third-party service providers; and conducts hiring and training of on-site staff. We work with them to understand and address their maintenance and long-term planning needs through our network of qualified vendors and even our own Associa OnCall maintenance team. This ensures that qualified professionals meet all our clients' short- and long-term needs. Our experience related to facilities management includes landscaping, HVAC systems, pools, elevators, security systems, and other applicable areas.

Accounting and Financial Services

We offer a broad range of accounting and financial services to assist clients with the day-to-day management of a community. Typical services include accounts payable, financial statements, annual audits, tax preparation, homeowner billing and assessment receipt, employee payroll processing, late notifications and routine collections, bookkeeping, and budgeting services. Our fully integrated software package incorporates our industry's tightest security measures and best functionality. We keep our clients' financial data safe at all times and always available to them in practically any format they need. Our accounting systems and processes ensure our customers have their community data at hand so they can plan the important next steps to achieving their vision.

Integrated Services

Associa's value to our clients encompasses not only our management and financial services but also the wide range of value we offer through our integrated services to communities, namely, Integrated Community Management and Professional Services.

- Integrated Community Management includes all the services that support the day-to-day operations of a community. Examples include maintenance and repair, communication tools such as community websites and newsletters, and real estate leasing and sales.
- Professional Services are specialized services that are part of the Associa family of companies and offer exceptional service and value. Services may include insurance, document storage, and title services.

By offering these integrated services, we enable clients to meet all their community's needs through one managing agent. We believe our role is to be a holistic resource for those who choose to work with us.

• • •

Whatever we plan, whatever we hope for at Associa, we always consider our roots. Where we came from and how we got here inspire us to strive always to offer five star customer service.

SERVICE IN ACTION

One of Associa's long-term executives often shares this memorable experience with our people. It reflects our service commitment that occasionally requires us to prioritize the needs and interests of others above our own:

> *In the very early days of the company—before we had expanded beyond North Texas—a horrific freeze and ice storm hit the Dallas area the morning of Christmas Eve. If you know anything about Dallas, you know that our citizens do not deal well with cold weather. Consequently, there was a general sense of panic throughout the city. Because we were in the midst of the holiday season, many of our fellow employees were on vacation, so those of us at work were pitching in where we were needed, and I was working in our accounting department.*
>
> *As the day wore on, the temperature continued to drop, and by mid-afternoon we were getting calls from multiple associations about burst water pipes. It was clear that things would get only worse after nightfall, and we collectively realized that we had a long night of work ahead.*

We called our families to let them know we wouldn't be home as planned and then began lining up our maintenance team, along with several third-party plumbers, to handle the ensuing hours. We set up our conference room as "command central" and got ready for the long night of calls. As you might imagine, having a torrent of water pouring from your ceiling on Christmas Eve does NOT bring out the best in a person. In more than thirty years with the company, I've never dealt with customers in a higher state of hysteria than we did that night. (We had one caller tell us that he knew where our offices were and that if we didn't have a plumber to his unit in twenty minutes, he would be on our doorstep with his gun. So much for peace on earth, goodwill toward men! We made sure the doors were locked, called the police, and then resumed answering the phones.)

Throughout the night, we did our best to calm and reassure dozens and dozens of customers whose holiday had been ruined by this weather. We were on the radio dispatching our technicians and trying to keep their spirits up (and dispatching others to rescue the technicians a couple of times when their trucks spun out on the ice). Our work didn't slow down until late morning on Christmas Day when we finally were able to go home.

It was admittedly not the holiday any of us had planned—my mother still refers to it as "the year I missed Christmas"—but as we all finally headed out, we felt really good about what we were able to do for our customers. Not a single person on the team had thought twice about sacrificing the holiday or "having" to work. Even then, our culture of family spirit and loyalty to our customers was second nature to us. The days that followed brought many thank-you notes and even some flowers from grateful homeowners . . . and an excellent real-life story of the power of great customer service.

QUESTIONS TO CONSIDER

1. What industry are you in, and how has service changed in your industry since its inception?

2. What changes have you made or are you considering to ensure you are prepared to provide great service as customer expectations change?

3. How do you prepare to provide great service in the future while still serving your customers today?

CHAPTER 2

Our Clients and Customers

A customer is the most important visitor on our premises. He is not
dependent on us. We are dependent on him. He is not an interruption
of our work. He is the purpose of it. He is not an outsider in our
business. He is part of it. We are not doing him a favor by serving
him. He is doing us a favor by giving us the opportunity to do so.

—MAHATMA GANDHI,
Leader of Independence in British-Ruled India

We excel in community association management only when we recognize the importance of our dependence on those whom we serve
and welcome every opportunity to meet their needs and interests,
whether large and complex or small and easy. Like most service
companies, at Associa we have always been committed to and passionate about providing five star customer service to our clients and
customers. Our industry, however, differs from hospitality, retail, or
other service industries. Understanding those differences is essential
to providing great customer service in community management and
to understanding our service recovery process when things go wrong.

THOSE WE SERVE

While other industries may offer services and/or products directly to their customers, ours is more complicated. We define our clients as the community associations and the volunteer boards of directors who are elected by their members, while the association members (homeowners) whom they represent are their customers—and ours. To keep this relationship in mind, we use "clients" to refer only to associations and board members but "customers" to include all homeowners, including board members. To serve each of them effectively, every member of our team must understand the complexities of our relationships to community association boards of directors and to the homeowners who elect their respective board members. An additional layer to this complexity is that these relationships change frequently as communities hold annual elections, often resulting in many changes in board memberships.

As we strive to deliver the best possible customer service, especially in trying to exceed the expectations of unhappy customers, we never forget that today's unhappy customer may be tomorrow's board member—or president! Boards have the ability to hire or fire us, and our relationship with them reflects a business-to-business service approach. By comparison, we serve homeowners in more of a business-to-consumer relationship.

Boards of Directors

These volunteer leaders come from every profession and every walk of life. Their common interest is their investments in their homes and, for the vast majority, their opportunities to contribute to the success of their communities. As volunteers for a nonprofit corporation they have legal and fiduciary responsibilities to manage the assets of their neighbors effectively.

While many of our volunteer homeowners have extensive professional knowledge about finances, construction, law, and communication, they will succeed in their volunteer roles only if they rely on the advice of experts in community association management. That is precisely how our Associa team can help them make a positive difference and excel in their important roles of serving their constituents.

In our business model our client is the community association represented by the elected board of directors with whom we have an ongoing professional relationship. We strive to strengthen this alliance as we offer direct services and advice to the board.

Examples of how we serve boards of directors are listed below:

- Providing consulting on how to achieve the board's vision for the community
- Hiring and managing resources within the community
- Supporting the community governance process through meeting planning and preparation and covenant enforcement
- Educating the boards and residents about policies and procedures for managing a community
- Collecting the assessments and maintenance fees necessary to operate the community
- Identifying and working with vendors to support the needs of the community

These are only a few examples of how we serve our boards. Each community has specific requirements based on its governing documents and the needs of its members. As a result, our contracts and services will vary accordingly.

Defining our customer service for our boards begins with clear mutual expectations and insight into how we can collaborate most effectively. Our success in providing five star customer service is facilitated when we understand and respect each other's responsibilities and work within the parameters defined by our contracts.

Members (Homeowners)

In addition to providing this expertise to our board clients, we are engaged to provide services for their customers, namely, the members of their respective community associations. While these association members are in reality the customers of the association, we are contracted to provide services to them on behalf of the association and its board. As a result, we think of these homeowners as our customers as well and strive to serve them while implementing the policies and procedures of each community association as effectively as possible.

Members of associations, then, are the association's direct customers, and we are the liaison for the association, through its board, to its customers. Association members are defined as customers because their business requests usually are more transactional. That is, they may request certain documentation, an update regarding their accounts, or information regarding the association.

Examples of how we serve association members are listed below:

- Managing access controls to the community by issuing gate transponders and keys
- Communicating about common area maintenance activities
- Coordinating special events and community celebrations
- Communicating about account balances, late fees, etc.

It is critical to maintain good relations with association members by responding quickly and efficiently to their requests, as long as those requests fall within the responsibility and authority of the association; are in compliance with local, state, and federal laws; and also comply with the association's governing documents, board policies, and rules.

Additional Customers/Stakeholders

We also provide third-party customer service on behalf of the board to vendors, contractors, and professionals who have a relationship with the association. Our third-party services are within the parameters of policies established by the board, the governing documents of the community association, and state and federal statutes that govern community association operations.

Examples of how we provide third-party service on behalf of our associations are listed below:

- Working with an association's attorney on a legal matter
- Engaging multiple landscape firms in getting a bid for service
- Managing relationships with a contractor on a clubhouse rebuild project

If managing all these relationships sounds complicated, it is. The illustration below may help to clarify the relationships involved:

Associa's Customer Service Relationships
for Community Associations

These layers of complexity often are misunderstood or even over-looked by many community association members and management companies. That can lead to unrealistic expectations, miscommunication, and frustration on the part of the members, the board, and even the manager and management company.

Providing great service begins with clearly defining clients and customers and then understanding their wants and needs. Since we have multiple customer/stakeholder groups, sometimes we risk providing great service to one and poor service to another—all in the same interaction. Serving everyone fairly, timely, and effectively is a difficult balance to achieve, but we must do it. Serving all these parties toward the betterment of their community is our challenge and privilege.

• • •

Our clients and customers differ from those of other industries, and so must our customer service. That is why at Associa we are keenly aware of our complex relationships with those we serve. Meeting their changing needs always is our focus as we develop, offer, and change products and services.

SERVICE IN ACTION

One of our employees in our Chicagoland location shares a great example of how she helped her board achieve some cost savings that resulted in a direct benefit to the overall community and to association members:

> As on-site community manager who works at the property full time,
> I am always focused on how to reduce expenses for our community,
> which ultimately translates into savings for the owners. A key part of

that work is to always look for opportunities to increase operational efficiencies.

Over the last several months in the community I manage, we have undertaken several projects to make the community more "green." We've done this by replacing older fluorescent fixtures with high-efficiency light fixtures, installing smart temperature monitors, etc. This effort has been appreciated by the residents and saved the community thousands of dollars in a very short period of time.

These are permanent savings for the life of the building, and I know by identifying them and helping my community manage their money better, I am providing great service for them.

As a result of these efforts, the community has been able to add more social events for the owners to their calendar, thereby increasing camaraderie between the residents.

QUESTIONS TO CONSIDER

1. Who are your customers?

2. How does your industry differ from others? Are there additional complexities that make serving customers challenging?

3. How can you try to keep all customer groups happy? Is this realistic?

CHAPTER 3

Our Service Model

When the customer comes first, the customer will last.

—ROBERT HALF,
Staffing Specialist

I completely agree that the only way to keep loyal clients and customers is to place them first. It is equally important, however, to understand the contract boundaries within which we must interact with them.

OUR RESPONSIBILITY TO BOARDS OF DIRECTORS

Those who are new to our industry often ask why we differentiate between board members and homeowners and between clients and customers. I do not tire of explaining that we do so partly because at times our contractual relationships with our clients (the boards of directors of community associations) limit or define our interactions with their customers (their homeowners or members of their community associations). The result is that our community association managers can find themselves squarely in the line of fire through no fault of their own.

Our responsibility to carry out the directives of an association board and our relationship and third-party communication with association members can result in homeowners getting upset at us, the management company. When board members make decisions about fees and fines, for example, too many homeowners direct their anger at their community managers, instead of at their elected representatives.

As managers, we must first honor our relationships with the boards of directors at all times, especially when their members are upset by an action we take on their behalf. Implementing a board's policy, for example, often requires Associa as the management company to send enforcement notices, as in the case of a delinquency notice or a violation of association rules. As you can imagine, it takes a great deal of effective customer service to perform this dual role.

Being able to explain the process and our contractual relationship to customers is imperative to understanding customer service in our industry. We go out of our way to help homeowners realize that the process is similar for the majority of functions in a community association: The board of directors makes the policy, and the management company implements and communicates that policy to homeowners on behalf of the association.

We are best equipped to provide excellent customer service when the board of directors gives us clear policy direction and authorizes us to make decisions that comply with those directions. If the board of directors, for example, adopts a standard for allowing storm door additions to homes in a community association, we can approve or deny modification requests based on whether the request meets the standard.

OUR CUSTOMERS' EXPECTATIONS

Similarly, it's easier to meet or exceed our customers' expectations when the board's policies contain clear guidelines about issues such as other modifications; enforcement of rules and bylaws; and delinquent accounts—specifically, when late fees can be waived or when payment agreements can be accepted.

We view our interaction with the homeowner as a vital element of our success, though we're always keenly aware that homeowners do not determine the fate of our contractual agreement with the association. That role belongs to the board of directors. Our delivering anything short of the best possible customer service to the homeowner, however, could damage our relationship with the board. After all, board members are homeowners too. What's more, homeowners who believe they have suffered the consequences of a board's decision may seek the ultimate resolution of the situation by running for membership on that board themselves.

• • •

Our service model reflects Associa's commitment to providing the best customer service within our contract boundaries. Our team members welcome opportunities to exceed expectations but are careful always to honor the directives of association boards that define our interactions with our mutual customers.

SERVICE IN ACTION

The example below comes from one of our California offices. While basic, it demonstrates a manager's role within a community and illustrates how well it can work when a good manager works well with her board:

> *I understand the great pressure that board members feel to do right by their homeowners by reducing expenses, implementing new things, and planning events that improve life in the community. They desire to serve their members well and want to do almost anything to avoid raising assessments or cutting services.*

When I began to manage this particular community two years ago, I realized they had a lot of room for improvement and knew that my knowledge could help them. Upon reviewing and analyzing their budget, I was able to recommend some changes to vendors and vendor agreements. I met with each of the vendors to renegotiate their contracts and through those meetings was also able to meet new service providers who I could recommend to other communities I work with.

As a result of those negotiations, the community has eliminated any overlap in services and improved the quality of work, all the while substantially saving the association unnecessary costs that the board used to reduce assessment fees for members. After just one year as their community manager, the board president wrote me a note that said, "Your leadership, knowledge, and management assistance is sure to help us continue to improve our community." That felt really good.

QUESTIONS TO CONSIDER

1. Do you ever have difficulty managing multiple client and customer groups?

2. By differentiating your service, how can you better connect with all your stakeholders?

3. How can you ensure each group of clients and/or customers is being best served by your efforts?

PART II

OUR SERVICE CULTURE

OUR SERVICE CULTURE

The reason an organization can deliver good or bad customer
service comes down to one thing; what is happening on the inside
of that organization. To sum it up in one word: culture.

—SHEP HYKEN,
Customer Service Expert

INTRODUCTION

Anyone can claim to deliver five star customer service, but, in truth, this worthy goal always is aspirational. No company, even those with a legendary reputation for customer service, is perfect—nor do most claim to be. Regardless of the worth of a product or service, what matters most is an organization's culture, that is, the shared values and goals reflected in how employees work together, the atmosphere that is created in which to work and interact, the positive attitudes that are fostered in good times and in bad, the determination to resolve problems, and the commitment to exceed the expectations of clients and customers.

Part II focuses on the culture we nurture at Associa that can be emulated in any service business. Its three chapters highlight our mission and pillars, our values, and what our Five Star Customer Service Model means to us. They lay the foundation for how we implement our model internally and externally, which I describe in Parts III and IV, respectively.

CHAPTER 4

Our Mission and Pillars

You'll never have a product or a price advantage again. They can be
easily duplicated, but a strong service culture cannot be copied.

—JERRY FRITZ,
Professional Speaker and Trainer

Competition often is the driving force in business. Many may compete for a greater share of a given market, and some will succeed,
often by offering the lowest price or a unique product or service. Such
success, however, is likely to be temporary as competitors continually
change the battleground of business engagement. The only way to
sustain long-term success in business is to develop a mission-focused
culture built on a foundation of service and framed by pillars and values that are understood, embraced, and enjoyed by all and that result
in loyal clients and customers, despite the competition.

BUILDING ON OUR MISSION

Delivering unsurpassed management and
lifestyle services to communities worldwide.

An organization without a mission is like a team without a strategy
for winning. Success may be possible, but it is more likely if there is a

plan, a vision, and a set of goals and objectives. That is why everything we do at Associa is based on our mission, our pillars, and our values that all work together to build upon that foundation.

Our mission statement may be short, but it is our framework that defines our goals and guides our actions and decision making:

Striving to provide unsurpassed customer service to the associations we manage throughout the world is the key to retaining every Associa client and to satisfying the members of their community associations. We will realize our mission only if we focus on providing the best service possible to our communities and to our board members and all their constituents.

While a mission statement creates a strong foundation for a company, it can be achieved only by building supporting principles and practices that enable all employees to put that mission into practice. When I founded the company, I developed four principles that we call our pillars. They define our key focus areas and allow us to put our mission statement into practice.

EMBRACING OUR FOUR PILLARS

To continue to build on the house analogy, if our mission statement is our foundation, our pillars are the supporting beams that hold our company upright and help determine its shape. Although developed many years ago, these pillars have stood the test of time and represent the most current thought about customer service, namely, that happy employees translate into happy clients, resulting in overall company growth and profitability.

Associa's Four Pillars

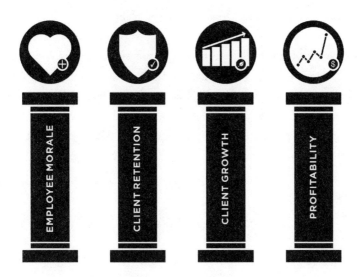

Employee Morale

"Employee morale" is a term often overused and even more often misunderstood. Dwight D. Eisenhower said it best: "The best morale exists when you never hear the word mentioned. When you hear a lot of talk about it, it's usually lousy."

Placing Employee Morale first among our pillars is not an accident. The key to satisfied customers is satisfied employees. It is that simple. I truly believe that it is nearly impossible for anyone who is unhappy with his or her job or company to deliver outstanding service or to make clients and customers feel welcome and wanted.

When employees have the necessary support, understand the value of their roles, feel that they and their work are appreciated and important, and enjoy the work they do and with whom they do it, our clients and customers reap the benefits. On the contrary, if employee morale is lacking, the customer experience will suffer, and resultant customer retention and growth will be at risk.

It is our goal every day to create an environment in which people feel valued and rewarded for their dedication to Associa and our clients and customers. I'm convinced that by starting with a focus on employee morale, we inevitably will serve our customers well. What's more, I believe that if we value our employees above all and understand that they are the key to our success, the remainder of our pillars—Client Retention, Client Growth, and Profitability—will be the natural result.

Client Retention

Retaining clients is our second pillar. Throughout our history we have led the industry in client retention, which is attributed to our focus on providing five star customer service. While retention is paramount to any company's success, it has become even more imperative in recent years. A happy client who stays with you also is likely to recommend you to others. Likewise, an unhappy client who leaves you is likely not only to denigrate your products and services but, in this day and age, also to broadcast that criticism via social media. Additionally, it costs far more to gain new clients than to keep current clients and potentially add to the services we provide to them. Simply stated, keeping our clients is good business—for us and for them.

Because I have grown this business from the ground up, every client loss is personal and disappointing. I hate to see a client leave for any reason but especially for one that could have been foreseen, prevented, or resolved. From time to time, for example, we have clients leave for perceived financial or cost considerations. If this is their reason, then we probably failed to demonstrate the value of our service. It has been proven time and time again that people will pay more for an item or a service they highly value.

Often a client who leaves because of price quickly will discover that the reduction in service and/or professionalism that comes with a lower price does not meet the community's needs. When this happens, we always hope board members will reconsider their decision, and, if they do, we welcome them back with open arms and a redoubled effort to prove our worth.

As their community management provider, our most effective and valuable role to our clients is as consultant and advisor, a role that differentiates us from our competitors. Our management philosophy begins with the simple philosophy of treating each community as if it were our own.

Community association board members and residents are more than clients and customers. They are part of our Associa family. As a family-owned business, we strive to treat every client as part of our larger family, and we work diligently to provide service, support, and follow-through. Retaining these clients through serving them well always will be a key priority for me and for all of Associa.

Client Growth

Client Growth is our third pillar. It illustrates our commitment to growing our company through effective marketing, sales, client referrals, and word of mouth. Of these efforts, I am most proud of the additional clients who join us based on our current clients' recommendations, for they are a direct reflection and manifestation of our efforts to deliver five star customer service.

Our desire is to partner with our clients to help them achieve the vision they have for their communities, and we are highly invested in their success. Since their communities are multifaceted, we have expanded our service offerings to match their needs. We know that unless we serve them well through the management of their communities, we will not earn the right to serve them in other areas.

Our focus on client growth also refers to our ability to provide additional services to the clients we serve through our various integrated service divisions. Just as satisfied clients choose to stay with Associa, those who are satisfied with our management services are likely to be interested in our other service offerings that are of value to them and to their communities. Interestingly, as we have interacted with clients and served their communities over the years, most of our additional services have been developed at their request. These products and services align well with our core business.

Last, our pillar of Client Growth refers to acquiring other management companies to add to our Associa family. I am honored to be one of the entrepreneurs who founded this industry, and I have learned so much from each owner and company we have added to our collective whole. Through these additions and our corresponding best practices, we ensure we are constantly improving our service level and learning more about what works in each market we serve.

Around the world or close to home, our success is most gratifying when clients express their appreciation through contract renewals, expansion of their services with us, and referrals of new clients. Every new contract we sign is an opportunity to provide great service to even more communities, boards, and homeowners.

Profitability

Profitability is the final pillar and ultimately is the result of doing the first three pillars well. I was twelve years old when family circumstance first made me an entrepreneur, and that is when I learned the value of profitability. Like many children, I started my own neighborhood lawn mowing business, and my profit was the direct result of how much my customers valued my service. I discovered early that the better the job I did for them, the more they were willing to pay and the more profit I realized. This was a powerful lesson for a young man.

That lesson has served me well at Associa. It is no accident that customer service is the cornerstone of our success. Our profits are tied directly to how well we serve our employees and our current clients and customers so that we can continue to expand and grow as a business. As we focus more on meeting the needs of each of these groups, we cannot help but be more successful.

• • •

As a company we enthusiastically embrace the four pillars of Employee Morale, Client Retention, Client Growth, and Profitability. As you can see, none of them stands alone. They all work together to build on our foundation of a culture of customer service. An inappropriate focus on one will lead to failure on the others, so it is important that we recognize their interrelatedness and act accordingly. Our success reflects how well we apply these principles in realizing our mission.

SERVICE IN ACTION

One of our managers in Hawaii shares a great example below about the results of freely giving of his time, effort, and expertise to work with a client after hours. His morale increased, he retained his client, and he created a win-win relationship for both the community and for Associa, demonstrating our four pillars of Employee Morale, Client Retention, Client Growth, and Profitability.

> As the first professional manager hired by one of my communities, I was honored when the board invited me to attend their strategic planning session several years ago. It was a two-day event, and I gladly gave my time. This has continued for the last several years.
>
> Attending sessions like these with my clients is the only way to really understand their community, to see what their goals are, to

determine how I could best serve them, and to help them to achieve those goals. Through our discussions we've identified several opportunities to reduce their expenses and add other Associa services, like our maintenance division Associa OnCall.

They also invite me to their holiday and weekend activities. I attend as much as I am able, as it allows me to get more involved with the residents, for them to get to know me, and for me to learn how to serve them better.

QUESTIONS TO CONSIDER

1. What mission establishes your company's foundation?

2. What principles build on your company's foundation?

3. How can you use the principles listed in this chapter, namely, Employee Morale, Client Retention, Client Growth, and Profitability, at your company or in doing your job, and how do these four principles relate to great customer service?

CHAPTER 5

Our Values at Work

*If people believe they share values with
a company, they will stay loyal to the brand.*

—HOWARD SCHULTZ,
CEO, Starbucks

Although confident in our products and services, our Associa family realizes that our greatest appeal to our clients is the values that we represent. Known as a family business that considers the people we hire and the people we serve as part of our extended family, we are committed to being a "best place to work" and the best community association company with whom to work. That is our key to attracting clients and customers and to keeping those we have, even dating back to our humble beginnings.

OUR VALUES

Motivated by our mission of providing unsurpassed customer service throughout the world, we have enjoyed building from that strong foundation. A few years ago our executive team went offsite for a strategy session at which we evaluated our company performance and updated our long-term plans. During that session we realized that, in addition to our mission and our pillars, we needed to articulate the core set of values that guide our everyday actions. While our mission and our pillars provide and build from a great foundation, our values frame up our daily decisions for our employees, for our clients and customers, and for our company.

The values we memorialized are not necessarily unique to our company, but they highlight the elements that are most important to guide and influence our actions. These five are listed below:

- Family Spirit
- Customer Service
- Integrity and Accountability
- Loyalty
- Innovation and Improvement

While only one refers specifically to service, all of them relate to our desire to serve each other and our clients exceedingly well. They are reviewed below, along with their respective descriptive summary statements:

Family Spirit

We are a family. We treat each other with kindness, respect, and encouragement.

It is always with pleasure that I recall starting Associa with one small client and many big dreams. As we grew in those early years, we added employees who had a key focus on customer service and who gave their hearts and souls to serving a handful of customers. We worked together, played together, achieved success together, and, occasionally, even failed together. Our work was not only important to us; it was part of who we were.

Each person helped with every job that needed to be done. We functioned much like a family, and that core value, Family Spirit, remains a cornerstone of our success. It means that we treat each other with respect and courtesy and want to see each other, and our clients, succeed.

I like to think that when one of us reaches out to a client or customer, it means we all are reaching out. Our clients are not served by one community manager but, rather, by the larger Associa family.

This value resonates with most employees and clients with whom I meet. Most people have a desire to be a part of something larger than themselves, and those who are part of our Associa family definitely are. Many of our employees say what they love most about their jobs is those with whom they work—their work family, if you will—followed closely by our second value, serving our customers.

Customer Service

We value our clients and understand that their success is our success.

It may feel repetitive to identify Customer Service as a key value in a book that is all about customer service. The key element we stress in this value, however, is that we understand that our clients' success is our success.

Providing the best service is always a new and different experience, because no two community associations are alike. Each board of directors reflects the members who compose it and the homeowners they serve. Accordingly, each board has a unique vision for its community.

Once we help clients determine what that vision is, we collaborate with them to identify and deliver the products and service they need to help them achieve it. While the delivery of that service may contain seemingly mundane items like distributing pool keys or collecting assessment fees, all of those activities are essential to helping them achieve their higher goals.

I am grateful for the opportunity to serve our clients, and I hope we never take that opportunity for granted. If we did, it is likely we would lose that client and others. We succeed in this business by serving others well and by realizing that our success depends on theirs. Clearly, the two are intertwined.

Integrity and Accountability
We maintain the highest ethical standards and are accountable for our actions.

Like all personal relationships, business relationships depend on a shared set of expectations and open, honest communication. Key principles, like doing what you say you will do and being accountable for your actions, are critical for success. While it may seem as if integrity and accountability are "givens" when it comes to conducting business, sadly, I have found that is not always the case.

At Associa it is important to ensure that our word means something and that our clients can trust that when we say something, we mean it. We believe in telling the truth at all times and, if we make a mistake, admitting we made it and then making things right. We then work to correct the problem and to make certain it does not happen again.

More important than never making a mistake is having the integrity to admit it when you do and the accountability to correct it in a way that surpasses the expectations of those who suffered its consequences. It is in the honest admission and subsequent correction of whatever went wrong that we will earn greater trust and are more likely to nurture loyal clients and customers.

We take our responsibility on behalf of our clients very seriously, and we know we are an extension and a representation of them. That is why at Associa we strive to approach every interaction with integrity and forthrightness, to set timelines for expectations, and then to meet or exceed them. We serve our clients best when we act in their best interests with integrity and accountability.

Loyalty

We are steadfastly loyal to Associa, our leaders, and our colleagues, and vice versa. Our hard work will be the mark of our devotion.

In too many industries, loyalty seems to be a rare quality. In a society that values instant gratification, it may be easy for employees or clients to leave when things are not going as well as planned or hoped. Without the loyalty of its key stakeholders, a company cannot succeed.

Our loyalty at Associa is exhibited through a commitment to each other, to our company, and to our clients and customers. We realize that loyalty is neither a right nor an automatic outcome. It is, rather, a commitment that must be earned, and we act accordingly. Our goal is to earn it by serving our employees and our clients well and by demonstrating our dedication to them, especially in addressing and resolving their issues. We see the fruit of that effort through the hundreds of employees who have been with us for more than fifteen years and through the thousands of clients who have chosen to be our partner for more than a decade.

By doing our best to provide the very best service, we hope to grow our Associa family of loyal employees, clients, and customers. We are confident that when they understand and appreciate our loyalty to them, they will reciprocate with loyalty to us.

Innovation and Improvement

We innovate constantly and always seek to improve.

Early on I saw that creating long-term success as a company meant constantly questioning the way we do things and looking for ways to improve. Over time, this developed into a core principle of how we do business at Associa.

Innovation and improvement often are associated with technology, but for us they are part of our mindset. When we see an opportunity to improve, we seize it. Often the improvement doesn't involve creating a new method, system, application, or technique. It may be a matter of simply seeing the way things are being done and making a change for the better. Our purpose always is to get better every day.

From a customer service standpoint, differentiating ourselves from our competitors occurs both in the way we approach service and in the way we deliver it to our customers. While our industry typically has lagged behind others in terms of technology, we realize that customers have the same expectations of us as they have of their multiple other service providers. The real-time, immediate response they get from an online retailer or food delivery service, for example, is the standard by which they judge our responsiveness. That is why at Associa we look to other industries to identify new technologies and new approaches to the way we serve others. It also means we must invest in technology if we are to continue to improve our service levels and to grow.

The driving force behind our focus on innovation and improvement is to serve our clients in a way that is faster and more effective than any of our competitors. We succeed when we align our efforts to innovate and to improve with our clients' expectations and deliver service in a way they do not necessarily expect. As technology changes and presents greater opportunities to change our industry and meet the needs of our clients, we will continue to respond appropriately and timely.

• • •

These core values guide our daily actions at Associa. We are determined to do our best to exemplify them daily to each other and to our clients. Occasionally, we may miss the mark. When we do, we will make course corrections quickly to ensure our actions always align with our stated values so that we can continue to serve our clients well. In fact, we ask our employees always to carry their copies of our pocket-sized *Associa Book*. It encapsulates our mission, vision, and values, enabling them to reference and act upon them easily.

SERVICE IN ACTION

One of our on-site managers in Florida offers an excellent example below that illustrates many of our values in action, including Customer Service and Innovation and Improvement:

> *A condominium building with an on-site office operates very differently than a community with a clubhouse and an activities director. In my building, we help the residents manage their day-to-day lives, including tracking packages, helping them with keys and garage openers, and ensuring assessments and work orders are handled appropriately and in a timely manner.*
>
> *While it may seem basic, an important aspect of living in a high rise is handling packages for the residents. At our site, we typically receive between 75 and 150 packages for residents most days of the week. With the increased popularity of online shopping, we needed to find a way to log packages we receive and notify residents to pick them up. Those packages may include their dry cleaning, FedEx, medications, or groceries (we even have refrigerators and sets of tires sent here).*
>
> *After trying multiple solutions, we now use an Associa online program that allows us to scan packages, print labels, notify residents, and provide signature pads for their receipt. This valuable service enhances the value of our management here and has helped our community become one of the most desirable in our city.*

QUESTIONS TO CONSIDER

1. What are your personal values, and how do they align with the values of your company?

2. How is a commitment to service evident through your key values?

3. How can you serve your customers by exemplifying your values?

CHAPTER 6

Our Five Star
Customer Service Model

Being on par in terms of price and
quality only gets you into the game.

Service wins the game.

—TONY ALESSANDRA,
Author and Motivational Speaker

Our mission, pillars, and values are at the heart of everything we do. They guide our daily decisions and give us focus when times get tough or the competition improves. To further build upon those concepts and to add substance to our goal of delivering the best service for the best products in the industry, we developed Associa's Five Star Customer Service Model. It captures the behaviors we must practice in implementing our mission, namely, *Delivering unsurpassed management and lifestyle services to communities worldwide.* Most important, they empower us to provide the kind of service needed to excel in managing community associations.

WHY FIVE STAR CUSTOMER SERVICE?

Our model is illustrated by five stars that embody its elements and action steps: Demonstrate Care, Communicate Effectively, Exercise Leadership, Build Relationships, and Own the Resolution. These points and how we translate them into action are defined and summarized below. How we apply them internally and externally is expanded upon in the seven chapters that compose Part III and in the six that compose Part IV, respectively.

Associa's Five Star Customer Service Model

| DEMONSTRATE CARE | COMMUNICATE EFFECTIVELY | EXERCISE LEADERSHIP | BUILD RELATIONSHIPS | OWN THE RESOLUTION |

When I think about five star service, I think about the highest level of service in the finest hotels and restaurants in the world. "Five star" typically refers to the finest, the best, the most impressive and unparalleled service possible. When we deliver service at our best, we anticipate our clients' and customers' needs, pay attention to details, and make them feel special. Our customers are not only satisfied at those times but also delighted—so much so that they are likely to tell others about it, whether in one-on-one conversations, at group meetings, or via social media.

While five star customer service is a lofty goal, it is based on our common-sense principles that are highlighted in our model and by our commitment to place the customer first. This means treating each client and customer with a personalized approach, identifying and meeting each one's needs, and engaging immediately and effectively in customer service recovery when things go wrong. Just as it surprises and pleases the clients and customers who receive it, this level of service instills pride in those who provide it. How we do this in general is explained below:

Demonstrate Care

Demonstrating care requires us to listen well, to empathize, to be responsive and sincere, and to help our customers understand we care as much about their problems as they do. More specifically, we demonstrate that care by our positive attitudes, by treating others as they want to be treated, by our proactive approach to resolve their concerns as quickly and efficiently as possible, by promising to find a solution, and by following through in a timely manner as agreed upon with the customer. We must remember that no matter how insignificant or irrelevant a problem may seem, it is important enough for that customer to take the time out of a busy day to contact us for an answer or resolution.

I have heard countless examples of our Associa family members demonstrating care, ranging from handling the simplest of matters to going to extraordinary lengths to serve their customers. Examples of the simple things include picking up trash in a community during a site visit and ensuring we respond to all customers within twenty-four hours.

More extraordinary efforts, however, require a greater commitment of time and effort. One of our community managers gave up her family vacation to help her community when it was devastated by a flood. While this is not an expectation, her unselfish act spoke volumes about her character and her dedication to the Associa family.

Caring for others can become contagious. When our employees witness their peers going the extra mile, they take notice and are more likely to repeat that type of behavior. When this is a company goal, it can become a key element of our service culture.

Showing that we care as much about a customer's needs, concerns, problems, and requests as he or she does also is a great reflection of our core value of Family Spirit and a foundational tenet of our Five Star Customer Service Model.

Communicate Effectively

Customers today expect instant communication. With the easy ability to send an email, type a text message, or make a telephone call, there is no excuse for not communicating. It often seems, however, that while communicating via multiple channels is easier, truly connecting with others seems more difficult. Regardless of the channel employed, effective communication can empower a person or a company to perform at a higher level than others.

Effective communication with a customer can be defined in multiple ways, but it ultimately comes down to two things: Did the customer receive the message you intended to send and, if so, in the way he or she expected or needed to receive it? Communicating successfully cannot be taken for granted; it must be planned, facilitated, and evaluated. By following up and requesting feedback from customers, we can either confirm we communicated successfully or determine pertinent courses of action needed to succeed.

When we meet the communication needs of our customers by communicating thoughtfully and thoroughly, they gain confidence in our ability to serve them well. As we express our commitment to resolving their situations and to following through, we convince them about our dedication, our attention to detail, and the seriousness with which we approach their concerns.

Often we can learn the hard way how important communication is to running and to growing our business. An industry colleague shared an experience that illustrates clearly what can happen when communication is not clear and precise. Let's hope the following never happens to anyone at Associa:

> *A community manager of another association management company made an appointment to meet with a developer about providing management services for a new community. While the developer was driving sixty miles to the management company for the meeting, the community manager was driving sixty miles in the opposite direction to the developer's office.*

The result was predictable: The developer had little faith that the management company could provide the professional discipline or attention to detail his property would require, and he went elsewhere for services.

The moral of the story? Ineffective communication is bad for business.

In addition to the day-to-day communication with board members and homeowners, it is essential for our community managers to know how to conduct good meetings, how to make good presentations, and how to diffuse conflict when it arises.

The ability to communicate effectively is not a genetic trait, which is why Associa offers communication training for our employees and tries to partner them with others in their locations who communicate well. We do our best to avoid miscommunication by helping our Associa family members learn to craft messages tailored for their intended audiences. Over the years we have learned the importance of understanding that "it's not what you say, it's how you say (write, text, tweet) it."

Exercise Leadership

If you were to google the word "leadership," you would receive more than ten million search results. There is no shortage of information about leadership and certainly no shortage of people who wish to be leaders. I believe, however, that we have a leadership gap in our society today. It is rare to find strong individuals who want to make the tough decisions and then be held accountable for the results of those decisions. As Wally Amos, founder of Famous Amos cookies, said, leadership is defined simply as "the willingness to pay the price."

Those who fancy themselves leaders and believe others should follow them merely because of their titles or positions often face frustration and failure. Leadership is a matter of vision, execution, and ethics. While our styles may differ, all of us at Associa want to be leaders in providing great customer service to all our customers, whether internal or external.

Perhaps because I was brought up with such a strong work ethic, my goal as CEO is to work as hard as or harder than anyone in the company to exceed the expectations of those we serve. These are values we instill in our leadership team and hope we inspire in all who work with us.

Exercising leadership on behalf of our company or our customers means there will be times when circumstances dictate the need for an employee to take charge. Regardless of job title, I expect anyone in our company to be able to take the lead when asked to do so. Examples of this include filling in for a sick peer at a board meeting, volunteering to serve on an Associa committee or to work with a charitable or civic organization in organizing or hosting an event, or responding to an after-hours call.

As leaders, we set the example. That's why I welcome opportunities to model my willingness to do any job. When necessary, I have taken out the trash, served refreshments at a board meeting, participated in brainstorming sessions, called clients directly, and responded to letters from unhappy homeowners. This demonstrates to our leaders and others my expectation for everyone to work in the trenches, thereby underscoring our commitment to provide the best customer service possible through actions big and small. People notice what we do more than what we say. They respect us more and are more likely to follow our leadership when we're willing to walk in their shoes.

By doing these things and others, we demonstrate leadership to our customers and to each other. Such leadership may be recognized and rewarded through the simple retention of an account or through other, perhaps more public, means. In any case, when we step up to lead a situation on a customer's behalf, the benefit will be both to that person and to us.

Associa is blessed with exceptional leaders at all levels of the company. Many are respected internally as well as throughout the worldwide community management industry. Some of them started in entry-level positions and worked their way up the ladder, largely because of their ability to exercise leadership when called upon. These experienced leaders serve as role models and mentors for new personnel and are essential to our success.

Build Relationships

Ask any community management professional what the key to building long-term customer relationships is, and each will stress that a foundation of great service and expertise is paramount. As a people business, we are keenly aware that our long-term success depends on the quality of relationships we build with our clients. When we continuously strengthen those relationships and treat clients and customers like part of our extended Associa family, they are more likely to support us when problems arise, references are needed, or contracts are due for renewal.

A letter from a community association board member illustrates how relationships are key to our business model and to retaining clients. The writer began by congratulating Associa's community manager for "winning our business back." Then she went on to say that the board had decided to hire another management company, but when a newly hired Associa manager heard the news, he quickly addressed any outstanding issues and brought to the board a multi-year improvement plan for the community.

The board believed his actions made their decision to leave more difficult, but they had already decided to go. When it finally came down to the last few weeks, however, they decided that this new manager had truly earned their continued business, and they reversed their decision.

"We appreciate his efforts and thought you should know what a valuable team member (your manager) is," she wrote. "We are looking forward to his continued efforts and superior results."

Clearly, the manager and his team delivered Associa's five star customer service by building a strong relationship in a highly challenging situation. As a result, we kept the client.

A long-term client in Virginia offers another example of the importance of relationships in renewing contracts:

> *After we managed their master-planned community for 20 years, board members decided to ask for bids from other management companies. It is not uncommon for boards to look for other service providers from time to time, but we soon realized that some of them were unhappy with a few aspects of our service.*
>
> *Because of our long-standing relationship and their loyalty, board members allowed us to submit a bid. During the research phase of the proposal process, we learned that their main concern was our management of their golf course. That was a simple issue and easy to fix. We talked to the right people and resolved their concerns, and they renewed our contract. Loyalty and a long-standing relationship facilitated our ability to continue to manage their community, and listening to our client helped us resolve their concern and make them happy to be managed by Associa again.*

We strengthen our client relationships through such focused efforts and lesser ones, such as attending an occasional community association luncheon or event. Being proactive about our communication also strengthens relationships. Unprompted telephone calls, emails, text messages, and updates can surprise our customers and help them realize the value we bring to their communities. When we focus on building and strengthening relationships, we retain our clients and lay the foundation for additional service opportunities.

Own the Resolution

Clearly, great service relies on our ability to assume responsibility for resolving a customer's problem and on following up when we need additional assistance to do so. Simply handing off a problem for someone else to handle is unacceptable. Owning the resolution means that the person who first interacted with the customer resolves the situation or stays in the loop to ensure someone else will—and later follows up to ensure that the customer is satisfied.

To demonstrate our accountability, it may be necessary to call (rather than email) the customer to ask if his or her issue was resolved. If not, we should make it our mission to pursue the issue until it is solved, advocating for solutions whenever possible and following up to ensure the customer's satisfaction.

We are accountable when we see an issue all the way through resolution. Our customers want us to care as much about their problems or issues as they do, so we must take every opportunity to go the extra mile to show them that we do.

As with other objectives of our Five Star Customer Service Model, examples of owning the resolution can seem small but have a significant impact on the customer experience. Consider the case of one of our accounting employees who was listening intently to a customer as she described a problem with her assessment. Over the course of the call, this irritated customer also mentioned a maintenance issue that needed our attention.

If our accounting employee weren't intent on providing exemplary customer service, he might have ignored the maintenance problem and focused solely on the accounting issue that was the purpose of her call. Instead, he not only resolved the original problem but also took the time to set up a warm handoff of our customer to our maintenance division so that she could resolve both issues with one call.

What's more, our employee didn't stop there: He followed up with the customer and the maintenance team until the maintenance problem was completely resolved. Our customer was so impressed with his attention to her needs that her experience with us was transformed from frustrating to delightful—all because he listened to her and was eager to own the resolution.

• • •

Our aspiration always is to exemplify Associa's Five Star Customer Service Model. Although we clearly set the standard for service in our industry, we are keenly aware that we are evaluated by those of other industries. That is why providing the best service possible is key to our continuing success. To excel, we must ensure that all our employees master our five points of customer service and live them out daily in their interactions with our clients and customers as well as with each other.

SERVICE IN ACTION

Sometimes our employees provide the type of service that reflects all five elements in our Five Star Customer Service Model: Demonstrate Care, Communicate Effectively, Exercise Leadership, Build Relationships, and Own the Resolution. One such example was reported by a manager in our Mid-Atlantic office who abandoned her Christmas vacation to respond to customers who needed her help:

> In the community management business we have to be available around the clock, and often the bigger issues happen in our communities on weekends and holidays. An example of this would be last Christmas. Of course, I waited until the last two weeks of the year to take vacation, and while I was away from the office, an electrical breaker box in a large condominium that I manage caught fire. The resulting fire left sixteen condos without power over the Christmas weekend.

My board president knew that I was on vacation and was reluctant to call me, but he had no other choice. Working together, he and I found an electrician who would work on that holiday weekend while we handled calls from upset residents. It was one problem after the next, and, in total, the sixteen units had no power for almost four days. We kept in constant contact with the homeowners who had no power, including posting notices and opening the clubhouse for them.

Once it was finally resolved, both the board president and the residents were thankful for my work. While it was tough to give up my vacation, it was very meaningful to be able to solve this issue for them.

QUESTIONS TO CONSIDER

1. What do you think of when you hear the term "five star customer service"?

2. Is one element of the Five Star Customer Service Model more important than the others in your line of work? If so, which—and why?

3. How can you use the five points in our customer service model in your workplace to provide exceptional service?

PART III

DELIVERING OUR SERVICE INTERNALLY

DELIVERING OUR
SERVICE INTERNALLY

It is not fair to ask of others what you are not willing to do yourself.

—ELEANOR ROOSEVELT,
First Lady of the United States

INTRODUCTION

Our ability to deliver five star customer service to our customers begins with serving one another internally—both within our own teams and across the company, regardless of department or location. We do not tire of emphasizing that no job should be too big or too small for any of us, and we certainly should be willing to do anything we ask of others.

I define internal customers as anyone who depends on anyone else within the company at any given time, that is, our employees, our peers, and our leaders. The fact that an employee depends on our company for a paycheck automatically makes him or her an internal customer. In addition, we become internal customers for each other as we work together toward our common mission.

Our leaders have a responsibility to hire, train, and coach the best people toward delivering great service. They also must live it out themselves. This is the foundation for delivering five star customer service from the inside out and for exemplifying our core value of Family Spirit.

The seven chapters that compose Part III focus on our best practices for internal customer service, particularly in applying our Five Star Customer Service Model internally; the roles of leaders in developing a culture of service; and how we hire and train the best employees, keep their morale high, communicate effectively with all members of our Associa team, and reward our service heroes.

CHAPTER 7

Demonstrating How
We Serve Each Other

Your customer doesn't care how much you
know until they know how much you care.

—DAMON RICHARDS,
Business Consultant

The best practices for customer service are quite simple. Many that we implement internally at Associa apply well outside of business organizations and did not originate from any business school course or management book. First and foremost, much like our external priority, our priority in applying our Five Star Customer Service Model internally is to treat every employee like a family member while reflecting our core value of Family Spirit. We show that we care about each other by nurturing a family-friendly working environment in which we can interact comfortably and joyfully, as if we were working at home.

INTERNAL CUSTOMER SERVICE
BEST PRACTICES

We know that when employees feel that we care about them, they are more likely to care about others, whether at the office or at the communities we manage. This is important, largely because internal and external customers want more than expertise and value. They want us to care about them by listening, by responding, and by collaborating within a pleasant working environment. At Associa we demonstrate exactly that.

When looking for the right way to do things internally, many businesses look for best practices of other organizations to implement within their own. They search for examples of how others achieved success in a specific area and assume it should be repeatable, regardless of company or industry. Certainly that is true of best practices in internal customer service. Just as we look externally to determine how to improve internally, we see how others, including the competitors in our industry, are emulating us. Their doing so is the ultimate compliment and recognizes our continual effort to offer the best products and services for our customers, whether internal or external.

Associa's best practices for internal five star customer service are not unique to our company or industry or to business in general. Frankly, the best practices for internal and external customer service revolve around treating others well. Being nice and being likable are good habits to practice at work, at home, or in the community. The business-specific examples that follow may stir memories of countless others that are just as relevant. They are especially typical of Associa, where our value of Family Spirit is at the heart of everything we do.

Practice the Golden and Platinum Rules

The first best practice should be familiar: Treat others as you would like to be treated. I learned this Golden Rule as a boy and found that as I continue to keep it in mind, the quality of my relationships with others improves, as does my ability to serve them. I also practice the Platinum Rule: Treat others the way they want to be treated.

Our employees provide five star customer service by not responding to others automatically in terms of their own preferences but instead by asking themselves questions such as, "How would I want to be treated if I were in that person's shoes?" and "How does that person want to be treated?" Customer-centered responses are part of our Associa culture, and they are at the core of our best practices.

Maintain a Friendly Attitude

Our second best practice is to maintain a friendly attitude. This is one of the main qualities we look for when hiring people to join our company, as it is critical to serving our clients and customers. We recognize that friendly people help build our culture, reflect our family-first attitude, and are more pleasant to work with in meeting our goals.

One simple example is how we typically greet each other at the beginning of the day with a "good morning," smile at one another in the hallway, or end the day with a fond farewell. As these practices become part of our culture, we create the type of company in which people want to work. It would be extremely difficult to have a friendly attitude with our clients and customers without seeing other friendly faces within our offices.

Respond Quickly

The third best practice is to respond quickly. I believe timely follow-up is a key to our level of success, and this applies as much internally as it does externally. This is why we have a rule for our employees, including our leaders, to respond to a client or customer request within twenty-four hours, and we expect the same quick responses internally with one another. While sometimes difficult to achieve, a timely response shows others that we respect their needs and is a hallmark of five star customer service.

Show Gratitude

The fourth best practice is to show gratitude. When we are thankful for those who help us and let them know, we encourage that helpful behavior to continue. Showing gratitude is one of the most overlooked skills in the workplace today. It is not enough simply to give our employees their paychecks; we also must give them direction and a sense of purpose. When they deliver on and act in line with that direction, we appreciate and recognize their effort and express our thankfulness.

A thoughtful practice that I learned early in my career is the value of writing thank-you notes. In fact, I send more handwritten notes to employees today than ever. Making this effort has become especially meaningful in our world of electronic communication. Taking the time to simply handwrite a note expressing gratitude shows others that we recognize the effort they put into their work and appreciate them.

• • •

These basic principles are reminders that good service is not difficult to provide; it is the outcome of good behavior toward others. Whether that is directed internally to our employees and other stakeholders, or externally to our customers and clients, these behaviors are the drivers of our success.

SERVICE IN ACTION

Our five star internal customer service helps our employees bond as they collaborate. Equally important, it helps them succeed in serving our clients and customers. This manager's report from one of our Texas locations is a perfect example of excellent collaboration:

> *While preparing for an upcoming project for one of my largest communities, I realized how time sensitive and complex the project was going to be. Not only was our postage meter machine, which was necessary to complete the giant mailing, temporarily out of order, but I also did not have the staff available to complete the project.*
>
> *I reached out to another local branch office. Their response? "We would be more than happy to help you with this project." I couldn't believe it; not only were they willing to stay late to help me, but also to let me bring my materials to their branch so I could use their meter machine the next day.*
>
> *Because we all came together to help each other, we managed to deliver the project perfectly to the client. I sent the other branch office a card the next week and told them, "I would never have been able to deliver on my promise to this client had you not helped me! Thank you!"*

QUESTIONS TO CONSIDER

1. What simple principles do you consider important to internal customer service?

2. Are these principles different from those you consider important for external service? If so, how?

3. Which of these principles do you believe is the most important? Why?

CHAPTER 8

Internalizing Our Five Star Customer Service Model

If we want our external customer service to be first rate,
our internal customer service must be first rate first.

—DEAN LINDSAY,
Business Speaker

Like charity, customer service begins at home. Before we can expect our Associa employees to provide first-rate customer service externally, we want them to experience and to provide it internally. Feeling that they are part of our Associa family is essential to their welcoming our external clients and customers to join our extended family. That is why when defining and living out our customer service principles, we begin with our internal customers.

Serving each other and being dedicated to one another's success is the result of the daily choices we make about how to treat one another at work. Based on our core value of Family Spirit, the culture of five star customer service internally comprises the collection of those daily choices that are as simple as the following:

- How do we respond to an email from a coworker, even on a bad day?
- How do we handle an unexpected request for help or information?

- How do we assist new employees or those assigned new duties?
- How do we treat someone in a different department?
- How do we greet others when we pass them in the hallway?
- How do we volunteer to help a coworker who obviously needs assistance?
- How do we end our day or workweek cheerfully?

It is in these little moments each day that a culture of five star customer service is reinforced or destroyed. We must first treat each other with kindness and like family if we hope to do the same with our external customers.

ALIGNMENT WITH OUR VALUES

We support our delivery of five star customer service externally and internally by aligning each star with one of our core values introduced in chapter 5. This alignment strengthens our commitment to each service star and creates a consistent message for all customers.

Associa's Five Star Customer Service Model
Aligned with Our Core Values

DEMONSTRATE CARE	COMMUNICATE EFFECTIVELY	EXERCISE LEADERSHIP	BUILD RELATIONSHIPS	OWN THE RESOLUTION
FAMILY SPIRIT	CUSTOMER SERVICE	INNOVATION & IMPROVEMENT	LOYALTY	INTEGRITY & ACCOUNTABILITY

- Family Spirit is the core of Demonstrating Care.
- Customer Service is based on understanding the needs of the customer and Communicating Effectively.
- Innovation and Improvement are the results of Exercising Leadership.

- Loyalty is the outcome of Building Relationships.
- Integrity and Accountability are demonstrated by our commitment to Own the Resolution.

INTERNAL FIVE STAR
CUSTOMER SERVICE MODEL

Because each person within the company is an internal customer, we revisit our five customer service stars to determine how to treat one another. Cumulatively, they provide a framework by which we serve each other, and the more we practice them internally, the more natural they become with our external customers.

This means we are committed to interacting with our internal customers by the same principles we practice with our external customers, namely, Demonstrate Care, Communicate Effectively, Exercise Leadership, Build Relationships, and Own the Resolution. How we do this is reviewed below:

Demonstrate Care

We first show five star customer service by demonstrating care to each other. I am keenly aware that in addition to the thousands of communities we manage, our organization is responsible for the livelihood of each of our employees and, cumulatively, of their families. I take this responsibility seriously.

When business is tough or difficult decisions need to be made, it is important to consider all sides of the issue and to show how we care about each employee. I hope that in every interaction I have with members of the Associa team, they can see the care I have for them first and then the concern I have for our business. This helps us address any necessary issues with the right perspective.

Communicate Effectively

Just as we want to communicate openly and honestly with our external customers, we also do so with each other. We must consider how we communicate a message and not only what we want to communicate. Truly, "it's not what we say, it's how we say it" is a communication mantra at Associa.

Communication within an organization is critical if we are to develop a culture of service. It is a key driver of Employee Morale, which is the first of Associa's four pillars, and is directly correlated to customer satisfaction. Especially because Associa is a global organization that comprises a network of branch locations, we focus on the importance of communication and develop internal systems and a culture that supports continually sharing information.

Exercise Leadership

We speak often within Associa about the "why" of what we do. We exist to help our clients and their communities achieve their vision. It is important to keep this "why" in mind and communicate it internally as much as possible. Our internal customers need this reminder frequently so that they don't lose sight of the bigger picture.

It therefore becomes the responsibility of the leaders within the organization to serve others by providing that vision, direction, and leadership to help our internal customers keep focused on their purpose.

In fact, five star customer service begins with our leaders. They are the linchpins in the chain to provide good service to our clients. We require them not only to provide the vision but also to execute it. This means inspiring, equipping, and coaching our employees toward success. Leaders must model the highest standards in their words and actions and show our internal customers every day the passion it takes to provide this level of customer service internally and externally.

Build Relationships

All relationships among our internal customers are built on trust. By treating each other as members of our extended corporate family, we encourage employees to get to know and trust each other and to build relationships. Because most people spend more time at work than with their families, they typically welcome a working environment in which they can socialize and have the opportunity to be part of a team.

Additionally, building relationships with coworkers helps maintain perspective if there is a dispute. The more we know about others, the more we can relate to them and the easier we can find common ground with them when we may be in conflict.

Own the Resolution

While this practice may seem more relevant for our external clients and customers, it applies equally when discussing internal customer service. As we do with our clients, each of us within Associa must own a situation and move its resolution to completion. It is easy within a large organization such as ours to assume that others will take responsibility for an issue. Instead of making such assumptions, however, every coworker should feel a sense of responsibility to resolve an issue.

Whether it fits within our job description, within our department, or within our scope of understanding, taking ownership of an internal issue or problem becomes our duty to each other. What we never want to hear anyone at Associa say is, "That's not my job." When we serve each other by resolving issues this way, we are all free to serve our clients more easily.

• • •

Applying our Five Star Customer Service Model internally is essential to our success in serving our external customers. Employees who develop the good habits of treating each other well will more naturally extend that behavior toward others.

SERVICE IN ACTION

Our home office employees are aware that their roles are to serve those in the field who have direct contact with our customers. When we do this well, we enable our field employees to focus their efforts externally, rather than on resolving internal issues. Here is an example of how one home office employee serves others and makes them feel as though she is an extension of their team, even if they are in another country:

> *Sarah has never let me down. Even if she is unable to help me, she will point me to those who can. She continually goes over and above in serving. She is the definition of Five Star Service. She is always willing to stop what she is doing to assist me; she puts the customer first.*
>
> *Even though we mostly communicate via email, I know that she is smiling as she writes it and I totally feel special. She is an integral part of my team; she just works in Dallas while I am in Canada.*

QUESTIONS TO CONSIDER

1. How important do you think it is to serve your coworkers along with your clients?

2. How can you use the elements of five star customer service to serve those with whom you work?

3. How do you see others serving you in this way?

CHAPTER 9

Serving while Leading

Good leaders must first become good servants.

—ROBERT GREENLEAF,
Founder, Greenleaf Center for Servant Leadership

Service in our business relationships matters more than nearly anything we can deliver. Serving one another, therefore, becomes how we create, build, and solidify relationships not only with our external clients and customers but even more so with one another. Before we can lead, we must know how to follow and how to serve others. If we don't serve one another well, we can't manifest that behavior—that service mindset—to our employees and our clients.

CULTURE OF CUSTOMER SERVICE

With thousands of employees and a footprint across the world, creating a consistent culture is a challenge that can be met only with collaboration, communication, and commitment.

The cumulative impact of daily acts that develop into good habits results in creating a consistent culture of customer service. This means developing an environment in which service is, like Aristotle's definition of excellence, not an act but a habit. Customer service begins at home, and it starts at the top.

The best kind of internal customer service is more than not leaving for the day before responding to our coworkers' telephone calls and emails or following up to ensure action items were accomplished. It requires deliberate intention to deliver five star customer service to those whom we are privileged to call Associa family members.

OUR LEADERSHIP MODEL

Many are familiar with the graphic below, which was developed and communicated in the 1980s: the inverted pyramid. Generally, the inverted pyramid is a customer service illustration reflecting how an organization might look if customer service—internally and externally—were its top priority.

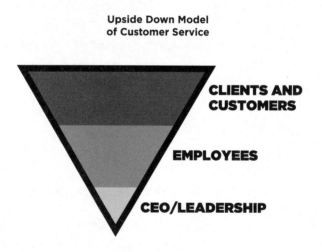

**Upside Down Model
of Customer Service**

CLIENTS AND CUSTOMERS

EMPLOYEES

CEO/LEADERSHIP

A typical organization is represented by a pyramid, with the CEO and leaders at the top of the pyramid and the employees and external customers at the base. The inverted pyramid above, however, represents the reverse of that structure: The clients and customers, whether internal or external, are at the top, and the leaders of the organization are at the bottom. This model represents well what we try to do at Associa, where our internal and external customers are our primary focus and most important participants in our processes. Our leadership structure exists only to serve and to guide those groups, not to be served by them.

To do this, one of the focus areas of our operations team is to visit our branch locations frequently and participate in "ride-along" sessions. This helps our leadership team see firsthand what it is like to be at the front line of the organization and keep the perspective of our employees at the forefront of their minds. By visiting our communities frequently, attending board meetings, and visiting one-on-one and in small groups with our employees, our leaders walk alongside those they serve and use the information they gain through those activities to inform their business decisions.

LEADERS SET THE STANDARD

We know inherently that inspirational leaders create inspiring cultures. That is why leaders at Associa are expected to create and foster conditions to deliver five star customer service internally through their own daily behaviors. While ensuring that the policies and procedures embraced by their teams support this culture, they are expected to model the behavior themselves. As leaders they also are expected to align the company's vision with attitudes, behaviors, and deliverables, ultimately providing an environment of customer service for one another and, consequently, for our clients and their customers.

What does this look like practically? Leaders are expected to serve their teams by living out our company values, particularly as indicated below:

- Leading with integrity, humility, and authenticity—always doing the right thing as they understand it
- Identifying areas of improvement

- Recognizing and rewarding employee contributions and coaching through areas of opportunity
- Encouraging collaboration among employees
- Reflecting a commitment to the greater good—loyalty

As leaders who put the customer first, we show up day after day to serve and to assist, not to be served and assisted. As illustrated earlier, we place the executive team and internal leaders at the bottom of our organizational chart, indicating that our role is to support everyone else in the company—to serve our employees and each other.

LEADERSHIP FROM THE INSIDE OUT

Because our business is a service business, I am acutely aware that our internal leadership practices will translate directly to our customers—even if our leaders never interact with them. The quality of our leadership translates directly into the quality of the interactions our employees have with our clients. When we are mindful of this direct connection, our organization can function at its best. The link between providing positive service-centered leadership and keeping clients satisfied externally is well documented. Dr. Benjamin Schneider, affiliated research scientist at the University of Southern California Center for Effective Organizations and professor emeritus of psychology at the University of Maryland, expressed this well:

> *There's a remarkably close and consistent link between how internal customers are treated and how external customers perceive the quality of your organization's services. A commitment to serve internal customers invariably shows itself to external customers. It's almost impossible to provide good external service if your organization is not providing good internal service.*

To ensure we are doing this, we listen, we build, and we lead through regular communication channels, including feedback from surveys and open-door policies. It takes the right people in leadership roles, however, to carry out and to embody our core values—particularly Family Spirit and Customer Service—in the hearts, minds, and actions of our people.

In short, service isn't what you do; it's who you are and how you do it, regardless of the level at which employees serve within the organization or the functions they perform.

I'm convinced if we can get it right with our employees—which starts with the mindset of our leaders—we'll inevitably and naturally get it right with our clients and customers. Clearly, our five star customer service starts from the inside out and from the top down (or up).

• • •

Everyone at Associa is expected to develop the habit of serving internal and external customers efficiently and effectively. Our organizational leaders are expected to model those habits daily, including by serving and assisting other team members, rather than by being served and assisted. This is consistent with our inverted pyramid model of customer service that places clients and customers at the top, followed by employees and supported from the bottom up by our leadership.

SERVICE IN ACTION

One of our employees in Colorado wrote to let me know of a leader she emulates who is a great example of how to lead through a service mindset:

> *I enjoy working at Associa. One of the main reasons is the people I work with on a daily basis, my coworkers and team members. One*

relationship that I value to this day is the one I have built with one of my vice presidents. She is the ultimate example of what a manager who works for Associa should be.

While under her leadership I have grown to become a wiser employee. She has taken the time to groom me as an assistant, as she too has worked her way to the top where she stands today, after beginning as an assistant herself. I am constantly reminded of all the times she has impacted me by being calm, kind, and professional in all aspects of the job. Her organized demeanor keeps me organized. Her excellent "customer first" attitude also keeps me positive and secure that my manager will help me get through the day no matter what comes our way. She makes me feel a part of her team, and that lesson sticks with me every day.

Because she works in unity with the different boards of directors we support, they too, in return, respect me. She has paved the way for success for me as an assistant. Her leadership is what keeps me knowing that someday if I commit to becoming a manager here at Associa, I want to be just like her in every aspect possible because she is first and foremost a genuine person, enjoys her job, always finding ways to solve issues within her capacity, and always willing to teach and groom a fellow manager or assistant all geared to providing genuine customer service.

The respect and trust that community members, boards of directors, and teammates have for her and vice versa is something that is dear to my heart and helps to keep me being the team player that I am today. To me that is what unsurpassed management is because she is a natural at providing the lifestyle services that keeps communities together, including our family here at Associa.

QUESTIONS TO CONSIDER

1. What role do you think leaders should play in building a service culture?

2. How have you seen leaders around you serve others and treat them like family?

3. How do you ensure your focus is on serving those with whom you work and your customers?

CHAPTER 10

Selecting and Educating
the Right People

If you hire people just because they can do a job, they'll only
work for your money. But if you hire people who believe what you
believe, they'll work for you with blood and sweat and tears.

—SIMON SINEK,
Business Consultant

At Associa, demonstrating our commitment to service internally is our way of life, our culture. Our rationale for this commitment is simple: When our employees feel appreciated, they are more likely to reflect their appreciation for our clients and customers by implementing our Five Star Customer Service Model. That, after all, is what makes us the leaders of our industry.

Ours is a service industry. All that we do hinges on the service that our employees provide to our customers. Offering the best products or leveraging best-in-class systems and processes does not matter to our internal customers if the person they are working with every day does not effectively use those systems and processes or reflect a desire to serve.

Whenever our Associa family must grow or change by adding new employees, we search for those who want more than a job—for those whose character and personality are consistent with our core values, our pillars, and our Five Star Customer Service Model.

HIRING TO SERVE

This commitment to service begins before our employees even become part of the Associa family, through the hiring process. We would not be the leader in the industry today if we had not been adamant from the very beginning about hiring people who are committed to and passionate about customer service. This continues to be a priority today, and its importance only increases as the Associa family grows.

I wish I could say that Associa had 100 percent employee retention and that we never hired someone who didn't fit well with our company. Unfortunately, we face the same pressures and "war for talent" as other companies. Finding service-oriented people who also fit into the Associa culture is not always easy.

To address this concern, we have implemented a structured employee selection process. It starts with creating and standardizing all job descriptions and related competencies across Associa. These are used by our recruiting team members as they seek talent for open positions. After potential candidates are identified, they meet with the hiring manager who is trained in Associa's interviewing techniques. During the last part of the process, all who have interviewed the candidates meet to review their discussions and to decide who is the best fit for our organization. This practice takes a little more time, but it helps us ensure that we hire only the best to work at Associa.

TRAINING TO SERVE

Once we hire the best, those new team members participate in specialized courses that prepare them to deliver five star customer service.

This is especially crucial for those who are new to the community management industry. The onboarding of new customer-facing employees includes their learning the expectations Associa has for them as well as the expectations of the clients and customers they will serve.

Additionally, all Associa employees are expected to continue their education and are provided with a myriad of educational opportunities throughout their careers. They can take advantage of this benefit in a variety of ways, some of which are listed below:

ASSOCIA UNIVERSITY

We spend considerable resources on our internal education platform, Associa University (AU), which we launched in 2006. This is our exclusive online campus providing on-demand customer service, communication, leadership, time management, and other courses to develop employees' knowledge and skills.

AU's original format combined courses delivered on our proprietary platform; on-demand e-learning; and a comprehensive library of publications, position papers, and books. From its inception, AU gathered content and courses written by our in-house experts and consultants and then supplemented them with licensed certification training from our industry trade groups. While its format has evolved over time, AU's foundation and intent have remained the same.

All employees are granted access to AU when they first start working at Associa and are assigned an individualized learning plan based on their roles in the organization. We then guide them toward customized courses for their respective roles, ranging from managers to maintenance workers. Additionally, many leaders suggest AU classes to their teams for further training and development after their annual performance review.

Our online learning programs include a comprehensive communication and customer service curriculum that combines e-learning with on-site mentoring and appropriate job aides to keep the skills in front of our employees at all times. This training focuses on our specific model for community management and is part of the defined learning plan for every community manager.

To complement this effort we have created additional on-demand education courses. Several of them were developed especially for new board members and homeowners and are available on demand via our digital channels.

Just as we look for the best expertise within our industry and beyond, we look for the best institutional resources available to train Associa family members. Over the years we have partnered with many institutions, including the University of Phoenix, DeVry University, the University of Dallas, and Degreed.com to provide a vast array of educational opportunities. Additionally, we have received multiple education grants through the Texas Workforce Commission. These grants, which total more than $1 million, have helped us develop the skills of our workforce and are a benefit to the larger community in which we work.

We are proud to enrich our offerings through our partnerships with these educational institutions to enhance the learning opportunities for our employees. Associa continues to look externally to highly respected colleges and universities across the United States and Canada to offer courses, degree programs, and continuing education classes for significantly reduced tuition and fees. To make this even more convenient, we connect much of this content to our AU platform. Access to these resources, coupled with their professional expertise and experience, results in Associa's having professional community managers who are prepared to offer advice a board can rely on when making decisions.

Our client board members also can benefit significantly from Associa University because of the courses we developed especially for them and for homeowners. They can learn more about their roles as leaders of their communities and about how to work effectively with association volunteers and Associa. What's more, they can access online resources regarding industry-related topics and learn about trends and issues in community management. This offering is very popular with our client boards. They appreciate our customer service model that includes these educational opportunities via Associa University, coupled with our in-person workshops for them and our managers.

Video Teleconference System

One of our greatest training challenges is to deliver our content consistently throughout our large geographic footprint. To meet this challenge we built an internal video teleconference (VTC) system that enables us to broadcast content to every location simultaneously. This technology preceded many of the web-based learning platforms used today and allows us to benefit from interactive exchanges across the Associa branch network. We train our instructors to facilitate interactive exchanges across this and other technology platforms so that our learners continue to remain engaged throughout the live-broadcasted courses.

Licensing and Certification

Continually educating our managers includes offering opportunities for them to earn additional licenses and certificates important to association management. While licensing and certification requirements differ in every state, standardized coursework applies to most certifications. Because many of our industry leaders also are national and international faculty members, we can deliver this material to our employees through Associa University. Every community manager in the United States can access it as a benefit of being part of the Associa family.

Evaluations

Instead of merely assuming that our employee education programs are successful, we include an evaluation component with each learning opportunity. These evaluations include course-related assessments, supervised role-playing, and direct feedback from our clients.

We also evaluate our employees annually to ensure we provide our best customer service to our communities. This includes our leadership team visiting our clients and discussing with board members how we can meet their expectations even better. We want our clients to have the peace of mind of knowing that we understand how essential our team and their service are to maintaining a healthy relationship among Associa, the board, and association members.

• • •

We hire the best people possible, and Associa's educational opportunities, policies, and practices make them even better—continually. Truly, continuing education is essential to our customer service model. Creating a culture of five star customer service is so important that it is one of our core values and an element of every employee's performance review.

SERVICE IN ACTION

Trusting relationships among Associa employees are based on mutual respect. Here's a glowing evaluation from an employee in Florida who clearly understands we hire the best:

> *Thank you for letting me share my thoughts with you about a true leader. It is one thing to be a boss, another thing to be a mentor, but a completely different thing to be a leader. Many people have influenced my professional life, and many have made very positive*

influences in my personal life, but one stands above all others. Educated, compassionate, and dedicated are just a few words I would use to describe our regional leader in Florida.

In the last few months he has shown me what a true servant leader is; he has put my and my staff's needs as well as the clients' needs ahead of his own. He has spent countless hours assisting me with client service concerns at our community to ensure a positive reflection on Associa. Ever since I began working under his leadership a few years ago, I learned a lot, which helped me not only to become a better manager but a better person.

QUESTIONS TO CONSIDER

1. How important is hiring the right people to developing a culture of service?

2. How can you continue to educate yourself to master customer service skills?

3. How can you take advantage of the learning opportunities your company offers to continue your education?

CHAPTER 11

Communicating with Our Teams

*Start with good people, lay out the rules, communicate
with your employees, motivate and reward them. If you
do all those things effectively, you can't miss.*

—LEE IACOCCA,
Business Leader

At Associa we certainly believe that great customer service means great communication. Why is communication so important? Simply put, it is how we connect and build relationships with one another, and that's what we rely upon in this business. Effective communication strengthens our capabilities both internally and externally. It may take multiple positive experiences to gain the respect of an employee or client—but only one negative experience to lose it. Our communication skills, especially relating to how we say what we say, must work in our favor—or they most certainly will work against us.

Consistent with developing a culture of customer service, we must begin with communicating effectively internally if we're going to emulate the same practices externally. Our leaders develop these skills over time. We help them learn to approach a situation with the other person in mind, which doesn't always come naturally. What biases might listeners bring to the conversation? How do we close the gap between the speaker and the listener? What form of communication is best for this particular person and situation?

Regardless of the answers to these questions, dealing with a situation successfully requires a multitude of skills that include listening, observing, sending and receiving appropriate verbal and nonverbal messages, and adapting.

BEGIN WITH LISTENING

Listening gives us insight into the other person's immediate needs, interests, and desired outcome. It also helps us understand not only what is said but also the *feelings* behind the words or information. It makes the other person feel more comfortable and confident that we care, facilitates a stronger connection or bond, and empowers us to respond more effectively.

Taking appropriate notes while listening helps us make a record of the important facts and reflects our interest and our intention of resolving problematic situations. It also enables us to ask the customer to repeat a statement, to clarify a problem or request, to confirm the accuracy of our interpretation, and to document any agreements about solutions and deadlines. This simple procedure is particularly effective in demonstrating our care and how seriously we consider the situation at hand.

Observation includes the ability to receive another person's nonverbal messages and to process that information in sending our own. We learn so much from observing body language—including gestures, eye contact, and posture—and listening to vocal qualities such as rate, volume, stress, and pitch. This sensitivity enables us to focus not only on the content of a message but also on its emotional aspects and on the ethics of our situation and of the persons involved. Especially when there is a problem, our employees should be prepared to cut through emotions expressed to focus on facts and on our responsibility to do the right thing.

Developing these skills is what makes us the industry leader. Our leaders can't expect a manager to walk into a board meeting or community and connect with our clients if they can't do the same at work.

Situations vary, and so do the most appropriate communication channels. Face-to-face communication may be preferred, especially when problems must be resolved, but this is not always possible. An employee who makes a telephone call seeking assistance, for example, wants immediate attention, making listening skills and sensitivity to vocal messages even more important.

How do we help our employees develop these necessary skills? Through education, practice, leadership, and guidance. Every spring employees undergo a performance review with their supervisors. In practice, however, this is not an isolated annual event but, rather, a continual discussion between employee and supervisor. The feedback they receive, both positive and negative, is one of the best ways for them to grow. I expect our leaders to engage in these ongoing conversations to ensure we nurture and develop the best-trained and best-equipped community management staff in the industry. After all, only through their success can Associa remain the industry leader.

USING EMPLOYEE COMMUNICATION CHANNELS

Growing businesses like Associa often face a communication challenge. How do we continue to connect with our employees while expanding into different regions of the world? Such circumstances require focus and attention to the proper and preferred channels of communication. Sometimes this means having a quick telephone conversation. Other times it means employing technological platforms such as email, internal discussion boards, social media, or a wide assortment of written materials. Occasionally it means boarding a plane to interact face-to-face, especially in significant moments of change, such as when we acquire a new company.

One example of this is our acquisition of a company in Canada. When we acquire a new branch company, our first and most important step is to ensure that the employees of that company feel they are a part of our Associa family. With that in mind, many members of our executive team travel to meet with the new company's leaders and employees. Establishing connections early is critical to a successful transition for all parties. Because we inherently know the best technology platform cannot create this sense of security and belonging, this is our standard process for all new acquisitions.

Clearly, different people need and often prefer different channels of communication at different times and places. Technology may prove most efficient in multiple settings, but face-to-face interaction often is preferred. I do not tire of repeating: Email is not a substitute for conversation. Every day we must have the courage to communicate clearly and effectively with our employees through whatever channel they prefer so that they can do the same with our clients and customers.

KEEPING OUR EMPLOYEES ENGAGED

Like trust, loyalty is a key ingredient in any healthy relationship. It has been the cornerstone of growing Associa and is one of our key values. Just as we are committed to our customers' success, we are equally committed to the success of our employees.

There are several ways we demonstrate our commitment to the Associa family and develop a deep, loyal, trusting relationship. The first is that employees come first whenever we embark on a change that will impact their day-to-day work. Before moving forward, we assess how that change will impact employee trust and morale.

If the impact will be high, we engage a team from across the company to communicate what is planned and to prepare everyone for the change. These team members help other employees know what to expect, and they are prepared to follow through with them to foster trust and high morale. As changes are implemented, they assist employees' transition into the new way of doing things.

Another way we demonstrate our loyalty and commitment internally is simply by listening and responding to employees' questions, comments, and concerns. We do this not only through the daily open-door policy of our leaders but also more formally through frequent employee surveys and company town hall meetings. We collect employees' feedback through quarterly "pulse" surveys. By asking specific questions about work experiences and how we can ensure Associa is a "best place to work," we collect feedback to implement new ways to improve employee morale.

We also hold frequent town hall meetings. These virtual, company-wide meetings feature members of our leadership team discussing the vision for the company and answering questions raised spontaneously or submitted in advance.

• • •

When employees know that they are heard, that their ideas are considered, and that Associa is determined to be the best place to work, they can feel confident that only when they succeed will Associa succeed. Above all, we want everyone to know that company loyalty is a two-way street. Those who are loyal to the company enjoy the company's loyalty to them.

SERVICE IN ACTION

To independently measure the success of our pillar of employee morale, Associa participated in an analysis of our workplace conducted by the Great Place to Work® Institute. The independent analysts anonymously surveyed our employees about many aspects of their life at work, such as our benefits, culture, work-life balance, and more.

As a result of that survey, we were delighted when Associa was certified as a 2017 Great Place to Work. A few of our survey results are listed below:

- 82 percent say that people care about each other at work.
- 82 percent say that they can be themselves at Associa.
- 81 percent say that management trusts people to do a good job without watching over their shoulders.

Feedback like this is exceedingly important to us. In this case, it was overwhelmingly positive, indicating that a large majority of our employees believe we are going in the right direction and that Associa is a great place to work. We care just as much, however, when feedback is critical or our employees have suggestions about how things could be better.

To ensure that we keep our finger on the pulse of our employees' satisfaction, we also hold regular town hall meetings during which we address their interests and concerns by answering questions that they submit anonymously.

When we hear about aspects of Associa's functioning and culture that we could improve, our employee advisory board and executive team continually work toward enacting solutions and shaping future strategy to address them when appropriate. We believe that listening to our employees and acting on their suggestions when possible provides them with a clear example of five star customer service internally so that they, in turn, are motivated and equipped to pass on that caliber of service externally to our clients.

QUESTIONS TO CONSIDER

1. Why is employee communication important to customer service?

2. What communication channels do you believe are most effective to reach employees?

3. How can your company improve employee communication?

CHAPTER 12

Retaining Our People

Customers will never love a company until employees love it first.

—SIMON SINEK,
Business Consultant

When our employees have the necessary support, believe that their work is appreciated and important, and enjoy the work they do and the people they work with, our customers reap the benefits. On the contrary, if employee morale is lacking, the customer experience will suffer, and resultant customer retention and growth will be at risk.

By embracing our employees as family members and applying our Five Star Customer Service Model and values internally, we demonstrate how much we care for them. We want everyone to come to work happy every day and to love to work here. When they love Associa and their morale is high, they are prepared to treat our clients and customers so well that our customers will love us too.

KEY ELEMENTS OF EMPLOYEE MORALE

Employee Morale is the first of our company's pillars that serves as the foundation of our success. It is first for a reason: In a service business, the only way to have happy clients is to have happy employees. I recognized this truism from the beginning, and it remains our primary focus. It is the combination of several factors, all with varying levels of complexity, and all have the ability to be impacted.

While there are numerous acceptable definitions of morale, I believe it is the delicate balance of five key features: recognition, work-life balance, leadership, availability of tools and resources, and accountability. These five items are the core of our efforts to maintain the employee morale requisite for our Five Star Customer Service Model.

My goal is to empower and encourage Associa's leadership team to embrace the key elements of Employee Morale. Because I am so passionate about this aspect of our Five Star Customer Service Model, we measure our progress toward realizing each element through regular employee surveys. These elements are reviewed below:

Recognition

Authentically recognizing employees for their loyalty and hard work is the most important ingredient in creating positive employee morale. Recognition comes in many forms. I have learned it is often the informal, sincere "thank you" that can make the biggest difference.

While keeping the informal recognition at a constant across Associa, we also employ a variety of formal programs to recognize employees publicly in a way that is important to them. One such program is unique in that it involves peer-to-peer recognition. The monthly "Hard Hat" award is bestowed upon the person in each of our offices who exemplifies Associa's mission, values, and pillars and has gone above and beyond the call of duty to serve coworkers or customers. Each month the current recipient selects the next recipient. Recipients are photographed and featured on Associa's intranet site as well as in other internal communication channels.

Another program was designed to encourage employees to understand and to practice Associa's core values of Family Spirit, Customer

Service, Integrity and Accountability, Loyalty, and Innovation and Improvement every day. All are encouraged to nominate the "Most VALUEable Player" (aka MVP)—an Associa colleague who exemplifies one or more of our values. The winner is announced each month via our intranet and in monthly newsletters.

In addition to these popular and appreciated programs, we recognize employees' special events, including birthdays, work anniversaries, and specific career or company milestones. One of the most popular examples of this was the celebration of "Associa Day" in 2012 when we launched our new mission, values, and long-term company vision.

Last, as mentioned in a previous chapter, I welcome opportunities to reflect the value of a handwritten note. I consider it a privilege to write to specific employees and recognize their examples of excellent service to each other and to our clients. I try to write and send multiple notes on a weekly basis, and I hope this small acknowledgment of appreciation for a job well done is valuable to team members who receive them.

Work-Life Balance

The topic of work-life balance has become prevalent, especially in recent years and among younger people. I have always found that balancing a growing business and a busy family is quite challenging, and it is something I continue to work through. Similarly, I am keenly aware that our employees deal with the constant struggles and sometimes conflicting demands between their personal and professional lives.

With the advancement of technology and the ever-increasing expectations of our customers, our employees are always "on." While this is not unique to our industry, the addition of night meetings, community events, and board and homeowner issues means that our business can be especially challenging for those who desire a true work-life balance.

To counteract this reality, we have implemented various versions of flexible schedules and work arrangements across our branch network. We recognize that flexible work is not appropriate for all positions or for all employees, but we offer it as best we can. Sometimes staff members have to work extra hours to meet the needs of the clients and communities they serve, which include nights, weekends, and some holidays. To counteract that reality, we try to ensure our employees have some flexibility built within their "normal" forty-hour workweek.

This flexibility usually is appreciated more than other company "perks," largely because employees recognize it as a demonstration of our value of Family Spirit. Without a doubt, we know this benefit increases the morale of our employees who enjoy the flexibility as long as their performance remains constant.

Leadership

We always are mindful that Employee Morale has two main components, namely, the structures and programs established at the home office, and the culture and leadership fostered at local offices. I believe each employee's Associa experience is influenced most heavily by his or her local leadership team, which is proven by data across industries. More than 70 percent of an employee's experience, whether positive or negative, is impacted by his or her leader. That is why we prioritize developing our leaders and helping them understand the importance of their roles.

Leaders at Associa often struggle to find the time to provide the requisite mentoring, training, and coaching of their employees, but these responsibilities are critical to employees' morale and to their overall growth and development. To ensure our leaders hear consistent messaging and receive continual development, we bring them together annually for a Leadership Summit. Our agenda includes updating them about company initiatives and strengthening them through education. We then ask them to educate their teams similarly by sharing with them the new information and resources highlighted at the summit.

We also have created multiple leader-specific communication channels, including monthly videoconferences and branded emails. These communication events give our leaders access to the most up-to-date information that they can then share with their employees and use to make appropriate business decisions. Keeping our lines of communication open with our employees starts with the recognition that the most important communication channel exists between a leader and his or her staff.

Additionally, we host semiannual training for our new branch presidents. These sessions allow the new leaders to interact in a peer group and learn about various company programs focused on employees and clients. They also are matched with mentors within the organization whom they can rely upon for additional information and guidance.

The impact of leadership on employee morale cannot be underestimated, and it is our goal to help our leaders be aware of their impact and have the skills to motivate their teams.

Tools and Resources

There are few things more frustrating at work than when you don't have the tools you need to be successful—or when the tools you have fail you. This can be the computer on your desk, the phone in your pocket, or the office in which you spend your time. I am passionate about creating a work environment that communicates the high level of professionalism that is the mark of Associa. We design the workspaces and choose the best possible and most appropriate materials, equipment, furniture, and amenities. I want our employees to have what they need to be productive and feel proud of where they spend most of their day. Equally important, I also want our customers to feel confident and to take pride in their management company whenever they visit one of our offices.

Additionally, we are always upgrading our technology, both hardware and software, so that we continue to lead the industry and maximize the efficiencies of our people and processes. We listen to the feedback of our employees and maintain the flexibility to modify our technology standards to meet their needs.

Accountability

As a businessman and former public servant I have always valued the following truism: What gets measured gets done. Under no circumstance do I want our employees to engage in work activities that do not have a measurable outcome. That is why we have implemented a performance review process through which all employees annually set individual goals aligned with the company goals. Progress is monitored closely, and a formal review of each employee's performance is completed every spring. Employees, including our leaders, should be clear about what is expected of them and how they are meeting those expectations. This annual process ensures we are accountable for contributing to the results we desire and enhances our ability to work together for a successful organization.

• • •

Even with the significant time and energy we spend making Associa a great place to work, I am fully aware that the best intentions and programs alone cannot be a quick fix for poor morale. We all have a part in enhancing how our employees feel about coming to work, and not one person or initiative can do it alone. We are a team. We are a family. We work together to ensure we remain the most successful community management company in history.

SERVICE IN ACTION

We should never be too busy to take the time to thank a coworker for a job well done. This boosts employee morale and reinforces good performance. The following is a thank-you note from a board president to a manager in Indiana in recognition of her delivery of five star customer service:

> *The most important component in any well-functioning organiza-*
> *tion is its people. Your leadership has become an essential and criti-*
> *cal resource for the improvements that have been taking place in our*
> *operation. And, I feel that people should be rewarded for trying to*
> *make things better! Thank you for being here!*

QUESTIONS TO CONSIDER

1. How do Employee Morale and Customer Service relate to your line of work?

2. If employees have poor morale, will they be able to serve their clients well?

3. What role do you play in improving your own employee morale?

CHAPTER 13

Rewarding Service Heroes

*If you're not serving the customer,
your job is to be serving someone who is.*

—JAN CARLZON,
Former CEO of SAS Group

Countless superb examples of Associa employees who provide great service are unlikely to be brought to my attention. I truly wish that I knew about every such instance, especially because I truly enjoy learning about our employees who excel in serving others, whether within our branches or in the communities we manage.

To encourage more of those stories to be shared, in 2015 we implemented a companywide recognition program called e3, which stands for Every Client, Every Day, Every Time. We present these awards monthly to employees across the company who go out of their way to serve their communities and each other.

THE BIRTH OF ASSOCIA E3

Every spring Associa holds a leadership conference to bring together our top leaders across the organization and to communicate and reinforce our vision, strategy, and annual objectives. In 2011 our theme was customer service. That was when "e3: Every Client, Every Day,

Every Time" was born, and it made a lasting impression. Although the verbiage was simple, the intention was effective: Serve every client, both internally and externally, to the best of your ability every single time.

e3: Every Client, Every Day, Every Time

ASSOCIA E3 AWARDS

In 2015 we resurrected the familiar mantra and launched a campaign to find employees who embodied the spirit of e3. We asked the leaders at each of our locations to find people doing things "right" and serving their customers and each other in line with our company values.

Based on those nominations, we announced and shared the examples of great service through all our communication channels. The success and recognition of selected employees demonstrated to others how they could excel too. What's more, these stories were summarized in key takeaways that we used in training and as job aides to communicate the importance of customer service. Many of the examples and stories you read in this book are a result of our internal e3 campaign.

At the end of 2015 our executive team accomplished the difficult task of selecting an overall e3 champion from hundreds of worthy submissions. It was my pleasure and honor to travel to surprise the winner with a plaque, flowers, and a cake and to thank her in person for her dedication to Associa and to providing excellent customer service.

The reception I received in that branch office was overwhelmingly positive and proved to boost the morale not only of the winner but also of her team members.

ASSOCIA E3 JOB AIDES

From the customer service recommendations we received throughout the e3 campaign, we created job aides, which we sent to every location as a "cheat sheet" and a reminder of our service standards. We asked employees to place these cards at their desks or in their travel bags to continually remind them of the first steps in providing outstanding customer service.

The general theme of the cards focused on timely communication that aligns closely to our Five Star Customer Service Model, and the message was simple: Never leave a telephone call or email unanswered, and even when you do not have an immediate solution, respond to the customer within twenty-four hours. We specifically emphasize the importance of providing this level of service internally and externally, as we serve our customers best when we also serve each other well.

Our Service Guidelines

e³

every client. every day. every time.

STAKEHOLDER	PHONE	EMAIL	IN PERSON
INTERNAL CLIENT	• Call back within 24 hours. Leave a voicemail if necessary. After leaving a second voicemail, reach out in person or via email.	• Respond to email within 24 hours.	• Display FAMILY SPIRIT.
EXTERNAL CLIENT	• Call back within 24 hours. • Leave a voicemail if necessary. • After leaving a second voicemail, reach out in person or via email. • If the client's voicemail indicates that the call can be delegated to a colleague, you may do so, but you are responsible for ensuring that this occurs.	• Respond to email within 24 hours, either directly or through an appropriately delegated colleague. • Responder should copy CAM. • You remain responsible for ensuring that your colleague responds promptly.	• Greet by name. Be respectful and professional.

DON'T LEAVE THEM STRANDED

PHONE
Your outgoing voicemail should designate an appropriate colleague, including their contact information, to be used in case a caller does not hear from you within 24 hours.

EMAIL
If you will be out of the office or away from email for more than half a day, set an out-of-office message. The message should identify an escalation path that the sender can follow in case a faster response is required.

DEALING WITH CONFRONTATION
If the individual becomes confrontational or hostile, bring in a trusted colleague to assist with defusing the situation. To avoid disruption, ask the individual to step into a conference room or office.

MINIMUM STANDARDS

• *ALWAYS RESPOND WITHIN 24 HOURS, regardless of your ability to solve the person's issue right away. At a minimum, you are letting the person know their communication was received and that steps are being taken to address it.*

• *If any communications relate to an immediate threat to life or property, every effort should be made to ensure an expeditious response.*

• *If any communications are received during the weekend, use reasonable judgment as to whether or not a response is required prior to Monday.*

CONTINUING THE ASSOCIA E3 LEGACY

Given the success of the e3 campaign in 2015, we decided to keep going and launched a revamped e3 employee competition the following year. To build upon the original idea and involve more of the employee population, the submission process was opened to everyone, instead of limiting it to leaders.

The initial competition recognized three winners each month: one from our home office, one from our accounting center, and one from each of our branch locations. Due to the overwhelming popularity and adoption of the e3 spirit, however, we increased the branch winners to three each month. Winners are announced in our weekly newsletter as well as during leadership calls and in other communication forums. As the program evolves, we continue to modify our frequency and number of awards so that we are always reinforcing the best e3 examples in the company.

Each month submissions of e3 excellence pour in from around the organization, and the number of nominations continues to grow. Employees relish the opportunity to showcase the outstanding work of their team members, and as the stories of customer excellence evolve, the decision about who should receive the award becomes more and more difficult. Winners receive a framed plaque and a gift card. It also is my distinct pleasure to send handwritten notes to these employees, thanking them for how they live out our Five Star Customer Service Model.

Everyone particularly looks forward to one of the highlights of our annual Leadership Summit, namely, our recognition of employees who excel in demonstrating our core values of Family Spirit, Customer Service, Integrity and Accountability, Loyalty, and Innovation and Improvement. The awards are more meaningful because they are based on nominations from peers at our branch offices, home office, and Client Shared Service Center. Winners enjoy not only receiving our Associa Value Awards but also being featured in our internal publications.

• • •

Rewarding our service heroes is one of the most enjoyable aspects of working at Associa. It is an opportunity to recognize excellence while reinforcing the importance of success in applying our customer service model internally.

SERVICE IN ACTION

At times, our e3 submissions involve multiple winners or entire teams who are exhibiting our focus on Every Client, Every Day, Every Time. This example is a great illustration of how a team came together to help our clients and each other:

> *Spring has sprung and homeowners are outside scrutinizing every inch of their units and calling our office to report each little thing that's wrong. Add in some heavy spring rains, and we have been experiencing very high call volume for the last few weeks.*
>
> *The entire Customer Care team in our office has been dedicatedly working to return every voice mail and email message in a timely manner, and have helped each other out when they get behind on their own email updates. They've worked overtime and kept positive attitudes throughout.*
>
> *In addition, many of them have made time to provide training and coaching to our newest Customer Care Representative on where to find the proper information for our owners and how to log it all correctly, and they've been encouraging happy homeowners to post positive Yelp reviews. This team does it all with energy and enthusiasm, and they are truly appreciated!*

QUESTIONS TO CONSIDER

1. What could your customer service "mantra" be in your department or company?

2. How could you recognize people who live out that mantra?

3. How do you think rewarding great examples of service translates into creating a service culture?

PART IV

DELIVERING OUR SERVICE EXTERNALLY

DELIVERING OUR SERVICE EXTERNALLY

Don't reinvent the wheel. Focus on winning one customer at a time. Be honest and sincere. Do what's right. There's nothing magical about this. That's been my guiding principle. To make it work, you have to live it every day. Make it your mindset.

—ROBERT SPECTOR,
Author and Speaker

INTRODUCTION

Our Five Star Customer Service Model is not magical, nor does it reinvent the wheel. It is based on simple guiding principles born out of years of interacting successfully with clients and customers in community management and beyond. Our goal was to develop a model that was relevant, meaningful, and applicable to what we do while capturing the principles needed to develop the ideal mindset for retaining clients and attracting new ones.

At Associa we accentuate the need to provide outstanding customer service to clients and customers internally and externally. The six chapters that compose Part IV examine our model in terms of how we apply its five stars externally to our clients and customers by Demonstrating Care, Communicating Effectively, Exercising Leadership, Building Relationships, and Owning the Resolution.

Each is so important that it merits its own chapter. Last, we elaborate about our multiple outreach programs that facilitate extending our customer service model into the communities beyond the associations we manage.

CHAPTER 14

Demonstrating Care

A little thought and a little kindness are
often worth more than a great deal of money.

—JOHN RUSKIN,
Victorian Writer and Thinker

Thoughtfulness and kindness may not cost a great deal of money, but
they are priceless qualities reflected in the first star of Associa's Five
Star Customer Service Model: Demonstrating Care.

DEMONSTRATING CARE

Demonstrating Care begins with our ability to extend our company's
value of Family Spirit to each and every customer. As a reminder,
we define Family Spirit as the kindness, respect, and encouragement
we offer to each other every day. By extension, Demonstrating Care
means treating our customers as if they are part of the Associa family.

It's likely that when you think of your own exceptional customer
experience example, you think about how you felt: "I was delighted!
They went above and beyond!" On a more concrete level, you probably
recall your satisfaction with the experience, how you felt at the end of
the transaction, how well you were treated, and how special you felt.

Then you start thinking about the little things: They followed up.

They remembered your name. They were knowledgeable. They knew your history with this problem. They paid attention to you and understood your concerns. You felt as if they actually listened instead of talked first.

Service like this is becoming increasingly rare in our days of technology and lack of personal interaction. That is why at Associa we look for ways to demonstrate our care to our customers, whether we communicate with them via the telephone, email, or other channel.

Those who develop the habit of expressing and demonstrating care are better prepared to deal with problems when they arise. Showing that we care as much about customers' needs, concerns, problems, and requests as they do is a foundational tenet of Associa's culture.

We demonstrate care in the following ways, among others:

- Being a positive point of contact
- Treating others how they want to be treated
- Caring for the community as if it were our own
- Being proactive

These practices are highlighted below:

Being a Positive Point of Contact

Being a positive point of contact begins with a warm initial greeting. The first time we pick up an incoming telephone call, say hello to a client in our office, or make eye contact is that initial greeting. This is when the customer service experience begins, and it can leave a lasting impression. Creating a positive initial experience consistently takes practice.

The warm greeting is but one aspect of being a positive point of contact. Other ways to achieve this, based on the communication channel used, include the following:

- Face-to-face communication: Smile, make eye contact, shake hands if appropriate, and use body language to provide positive and understanding feedback.

- Telephone conversation: Smile, listen without interrupting, address the caller by name, and provide positive and understanding vocal feedback.

- Email: Use a friendly greeting and closing, complete sentences that reflect ordinary lower case and capitalization style, and respectful language devoid of any humor or sarcasm that could be misinterpreted or offensive.

While these actions seem simple, such common courtesies make the difference in customer service. One of our clients offered the following wonderful example about the importance of communication courtesies as a tool for Demonstrating Care:

I am writing you to explain a situation I had when visiting one of your offices in California. I had only been a homeowner in an Associa community for a short period of time when I realized my bill was due that day or it would be late. Knowing I could not send it by mail, I got into my car to drive to your office.

Since I'm in California, outrageous traffic is a norm for me and by the time I reached your office it was two minutes until closing time and I was highly frustrated. As I was coming through the door, they were shutting off the lights and transferring the phones. However, your receptionist greeted me with the warmest smile and made me feel better instantly.

As I explained my situation, she listened patiently and helped ensure I wrote my payment correctly. She was friendly, and she stayed with me after her scheduled work time to make sure I would know how to send my payment in in the future. I was grateful for her warm demeanor and her kindness. She is an asset to your company!

This is a perfect example of Demonstrating Care by extending a warm initial greeting and following up with a friendly interaction. Our receptionist, through her simple kindness and patience, made this homeowner feel at ease and helped her resolve her payment issues. Based on the letter I received afterward, I am confident that her effort led to a loyal customer.

Treating Others How They Want to Be Treated

Many years ago Robert Fulghum's best-selling *All I Really Need to Know I Learned in Kindergarten* was embraced widely, even in the business community. As the CEO of an international company, I cannot agree completely—I certainly didn't learn corporate finance in kindergarten! I do, however, agree with many of its fundamentals, especially regarding how we should play (and work) well together.

Indeed, the lessons we learn as children about treating others as we would want to be treated serve us well as we move into adulthood and certainly for those of us who move into the service business. This Golden Rule and its variations are a great lesson for us to internalize and offer guidance about how we should treat our customers. That is why the following are highlighted in our customer service and communication courses for our Associa team:

- **Golden Rule:** Do unto others as you would have them do unto you.
- **Platinum Rule:** Do unto others as they would have you do unto them.
- **Other People's Shoes Rule:** Treat others the way you would like to be treated if you were in their shoes.

The best known of these is the Golden Rule, but using it can be problematic. If you treat other persons the way you would like to be treated, you might miss the mark. What if, for example, to appease an unhappy customer, you sent him a gift card to your favorite steakhouse, oblivious to his being a vegetarian? Similarly, what if you sent magnificent flowers to an irate customer who was allergic to them? Such situations underscore the superiority of the Platinum Rule—to treat customers the way *they* want to be treated.

On a related note, imagine yourself interacting with a rude, hostile, irate customer. Would it be helpful to employ the Other People's Shoes Rule? This would motivate you to consider the circumstances of the other person before responding and to think, "If I were in his or her shoes, how would I want to be treated, and what would satisfy me or exceed my expectations?"

By honoring these rules, we facilitate effective interactions and put our focus on serving others and meeting them where they are. We exceed expectations by considering our clients' perspectives and goals before we determine how to exceed their expectations.

Here is an example of how one of our managers put this concept into practice in her community. The treasurer of her community's board witnessed her serving a homeowner in this way and sent me a note about it:

> I wanted to relay an event that I saw at our complex yesterday. A car was parked in front of the social room, and a woman with no raincoat or umbrella was helping an elderly woman who had fallen to the sidewalk get into a car.
>
> She was drenched by the rain, but this didn't stop her from helping the woman. I called over to our hero and said, "You are a great human being because of what you just did." In today's world most people would have looked the other way, but not our community manager!

Upon reading this I wondered if our manager knowingly employed the Golden Rule, the Platinum Rule, or the Other

People's Shoes Rule. Regardless, this example seemed to embody each of them. These types of scenarios allow us to demonstrate care to our clients and to strengthen our relationships with our communities and their residents.

Treating a Community as if It's Our Own

An extension of the Golden Rule in our business is treating the community as if it's our own. Most of us can relate to the pride we feel in our home or our community and the desire to see that community flourish. We try to keep this perspective in mind as we serve each of our clients, especially because we know how important their community is to them. To do so, we must ask ourselves how we would want our community to be managed, what lifestyle or capital improvements would be important, and how we would want our finances to be managed. With these thoughts in mind, we can offer our best recommendations to our boards and make good decisions when it comes to the vendors we endorse and select.

There are also many ways that we can treat the community as if it is our own in the course of our daily management practices. Some examples follow:

+ We promote value in our purchasing decisions and are prudent when managing the association's budget.
+ We are aware of conditions that create a potential liability to the community and are proactive in making recommendations to maintain the common area.
+ We pay attention to the little things like picking up trash in the common areas and making sure that the clubhouse is secured at the end of the board meeting.

Additionally, at times we must serve our clients after an unplanned event or natural disaster. With justified pride I have heard many stories of our managers going to great lengths to serve their communities and help the residents return to normalcy after terrible storms, fires, or other emergencies. In Chicago, for example, a residential building we manage suffered a massive fire. One of our branch leaders emailed me about how our manager demonstrated great care in the wake of that tragedy:

> *While working on the restoration of a severely fire damaged building for Associa Chicagoland, one of our managers noticed a visibly distraught homeowner who had not been able to retrieve an irreplaceable family heirloom prior to evacuating. He listened to the homeowner's description of the item and did not hesitate to safely search the owner's destroyed home. He was able to retrieve the item, and the homeowner was relieved and grateful, as nearly all of their other possessions were a total loss in the fire.*
>
> *This manager's calming presence, compassion for the homeowner, and his willingness to take action above and beyond his normal duties clearly demonstrate his commitment to excellence in customer service.*

I certainly agree!

Being Proactive

Being proactive certainly is one of the most important traits of successful people. Admittedly, we often are too busy to think ahead and to take care of things before they become emergencies. It is critical to Associa's success, however, that we make the time to serve our clients by thinking ahead and helping them avoid problems. Proactive community management is foundational to our business model and to our quest to offer five star customer service.

In everything from performing property inspections to answering homeowner emails, we must ask ourselves as often as necessary,

"What is the true issue here?" How can I serve this community by solving the current issue and precluding a future issue? In this way, we demonstrate care by helping our communities and boards plan for the future instead of dealing only with the present. It is one way in which we help our customers live out our brand promise of helping them achieve their vision.

Our proactive approach also is about taking action when we see a problem, rather than waiting for a customer to identify it for us and tell us how to solve it. We take care of solvable problems or, alternatively, identify multiple possible solutions and approach our customer with options. My point is that good service is not about waiting for the customer to come to you; it's about taking action, the sooner, the better.

Being proactive also prevents our being in perpetual "firefighting" mode. If we merely are moving from one emergency to another, we are underserving our client while burning ourselves out. If, however, we can find time each day to think and act proactively, we likely may prevent some emergencies.

I recently received a letter from one of our board members who offered the following example of how our manager was proactive in helping their community:

> Our property manager recently was on-site performing his regular duties and heard a really loud banging noise coming from one of the other condominium units. It was so loud he was concerned that there was an issue with the unit that was causing property damage.
>
> After contacting the owner and entering the unit, he found the toilet pipes rattling, broken, and leaking in the bathroom. Due to his quick observation and attention to detail, he was able to prevent a real disaster and saved the owner the expense and frustration of having to repair extensive damages.

This is an excellent example of how being proactive can preclude additional emergencies and enhance our level of service to our clients. Demonstrating Care includes these and so many other traits, but it boils down to the simple concept of treating others well. That may be rare in some businesses today, but at Associa we consider it more critical than ever. Doing these simple things creates an ongoing connection with the customer and establishes the tone for all other interactions.

• • •

By continually demonstrating that we care, we add value to our products and services. Our taking the time to be thoughtful, helpful, compassionate, and respectful makes our clients and customers feel appreciated and understood. Cumulatively, our small acts of kindness and sincere expressions of interest and concern contribute to our culture of customer service. Those who know we care are more likely to enjoy doing business with us.

SERVICE IN ACTION

While in this chapter I shared many examples of how we demonstrate care, it's my pleasure to share one more that incorporates all the factors we discussed. One of our branch presidents in Florida reported the following:

> Just recently, one of our on-site maintenance personnel called the branch to say that he was stuck in the on-site elevator with a resident and could not contact the elevator maintenance company.
> While one of our assistants contacted the vendor, one of our community managers jumped in his car and headed to the property to assist our maintenance employee and the resident. We then worked with the elevator company to ensure we solved the root issue of the

elevator problem so this wouldn't happen to more residents. This stellar service was no surprise as our team always comes together to better serve each other and our clients.

QUESTIONS TO CONSIDER

1. In your previous interactions as a customer, how have other companies demonstrated care to you?

2. How have you been able to put yourself in your customer's shoes or used another of our three customer service rules to deal with an unhappy customer? How did that change your interaction with him or her?

3. What are some examples of how you can demonstrate care in your everyday interactions with your customers?

CHAPTER 15

Communicating with Customers

Open, honest communication is the best foundation for any
relationship, but remember at the end of the day it's not what you say
or what you do, but how you make people feel that matters most.

—TONY HSIEH,
Entrepreneur and Venture Capitalist

Excellent communication is the hallmark of our Five Star Customer
Service Model. This means concentrating not only on what we say
and do but also on how we say or do it. We think beyond the content
of our message to focus on how we can make our clients and customers feel good about it.

COMMUNICATING EFFECTIVELY

At Associa we understand that to communicate effectively, we must
craft our message for our specific audience and occasion. Instead
of simply focusing on what we want to say and why, we make sure
we communicate in a way that highlights the needs and interests of
our clients and customers. We speak, write, and present specifically
for those with whom we interact, and we listen and read carefully
and sensitively to them before responding. Indeed, our Five Star

Customer Service Model requires us to be proactive, not reactive, communicators.

When we communicate deliberately and thoroughly, customers gain confidence in our ability to meet their needs. When we are successful in expressing our commitment to resolving situations and to following through, we help convince our customers of our dedication to them, our attention to detail on their behalf, and the seriousness with which we approach their concerns.

Actually, communication might be the most important part of our jobs. We share information regularly via multiple channels, all with the intent of reaching our clients and customers with important and timely information. We also welcome every opportunity to build our relationships with them through additional channels of communication. Above all, we realize that we communicate continuously through our words and actions. The alternative, not responding, also is a communication—a negative one.

KNOWING OUR AUDIENCE

Instead of being self-centered communicators who simply focus on what we want to say and how we want to say it, we begin our communication by determining with whom we will interact, for what purpose, and in what setting. We begin by identifying the key attributes of our audience:

- Who are they?
- What are their needs and interests?
- What do they need and expect?
- What communication channels do they prefer?
- What is their experience level with the topic?
- What do we have in common, and how do we differ?

- How can I adapt to them?
- Are there areas of potential agreement or disagreement?
- What additional questions are they likely to have, and how can I answer them proactively?

Our audiences include homeowners who call with questions, visitors to our offices, vendors with proposals, team members whose duties are directly or indirectly related to our jobs, and many others. Regardless of who our audience is for a specific communication, our standards are the same: Adapt to them, and strive to meet their specific needs while exceeding their expectations.

The following are communication situations and audiences that our managers typically face:

- Our manager must prepare and present a report for a community association monthly or annual board meeting. To serve as many board members as possible, he submits a written report with an executive summary but also prepares a presentation that highlights its contents and lays the foundation from which they can ask questions.
- A homeowner is uncomfortable with the behavior of one of the board members and wants her concerns addressed during the next open board meeting. Recognizing that the behavior in question is more of a misunderstanding than anything else and to prevent a personality conflict from escalating unnecessarily, our manager suggests and arranges for the homeowner and board member to meet with her prior to the board meeting in an effort to resolve the issue privately and appropriately.

In the cases described above, the manager in the first example adapted to the preferences of his audience, while the second persuaded the parties to address a smaller audience in private, rather than the larger audience gathered for a board meeting. Truly, audience analysis facilitates adapting to, and planning for, effective communication.

COMMUNICATING VERBALLY
AND NONVERBALLY

Effective communication is more than speaking or writing effectively; it also requires adapting our message as a result of listening and responding effectively. We watch body language, look for micro-expressions, listen to vocal qualities, and try to adapt accordingly. We follow up with questions that help us understand our customer's or team member's perspective and how we can exceed expectations in our response.

We regularly remind our team, "It's not what we say, it's how we say it." This popular statement is based on research by Albert Mehrabian, a behavioral scientist. He found that the communication of feeling (not of information) is based upon 7 percent verbal content, whether written or oral; 38 percent vocal aspects (rate, volume, stress, pitch, quality); and 55 percent nonverbal behavior (facial expressions, gestures, appearance, posture, attitude, behavior, composure, movement, etc.). Our Associa employees strive to communicate effectively, not only by sending favorable verbal, vocal, and nonverbal messages but also by observing and responding to those sent by others, including while we're talking.

Mehrabian's findings are illustrated below:

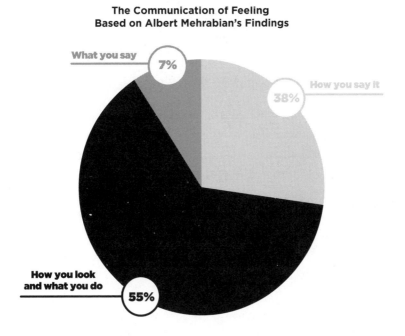

The Communication of Feeling
Based on Albert Mehrabian's Findings

What you say — 7%

How you say it — 38%

How you look and what you do — 55%

Note that the diagram indicates that 93 percent of the communication of feeling depends on how you say something (vocal) and how you look and what you do (nonverbal) while you say it. During telephone conversations, absent body language, how you say it accounts for 93 percent of how a listener will feel at the end of the conversation.

This is significant. In interpersonal settings, if someone's words and nonverbal behavior are not in sync, he or she inadvertently could take a positive message and make it a negative. If a manager, for example, reports saving the association significant funds after examining its insurance policies but talks with her hands in her pockets, her eyes darting around, and her voice sounding depressed and barely audible, the board is unlikely to believe her message. At a minimum, her communication would lose its intended impact.

At Associa we offer our managers training that covers all aspects of verbal, vocal, and nonverbal communication, ranging from listening effectively to clients and customers in interpersonal settings to developing packets for and presenting reports at board meetings.

Providing Accurate Reports

Another best practice in communication includes developing helpful, user-friendly reports, commonly referred to as "board packets," and delivering them to board members in advance of a board meeting so they can prepare ahead of time and have their questions prepared or answered before the meeting. These can be delivered via email or online through our technology platform, and we also give the boards an option to have printed materials for the live meeting.

These packets include all our standard information about financials and community activities, along with the optional materials that board members request. Sending these materials or making them available online ahead of time allows our board members to ask questions before the meetings to ensure the live meeting is run efficiently and effectively.

Service in many ongoing relationships relies on our ability to report to the customer the results of a project, the financial status of a community, or the documented decisions made by the board. In any industry, reports can be a great medium to deliver service by providing information. It's also a great way to record the work done for a client.

Technology, including smartphones and tablets, facilitates communication in real time. The result is that many times we or our clients and customers prefer to discuss important information right away, rather than wait until the next board meeting. Determining which information can be held and which should be disseminated just before a meeting should be vetted with board members and noted in their board meeting minutes.

Responding Timely

Our effective communication goals extend far beyond managers interacting with board members. Within our five star customer service guidelines, answering telephone calls and emails promptly and appropriately is equally important, as is handling maintenance requests swiftly and satisfactorily. With more and more ways to communicate today, the volume can be overwhelming. In our offices, each employee utilizes telephones, email, text messaging, social media, and instant messaging. While each communication channel has its value, without a solid plan, the combination can lead to gridlock. That is why we adopted guidelines for response times and methods.

Our communication guidelines begin by establishing some simple rules for nonemergency calls. These procedures ensure that each customer receives a timely response to his or her request.

To begin with, each Associa office has a system for addressing property emergency situations at all hours, every day of the year. Beyond that, our response guidelines require that for items received before noon, we respond by the end of the business day, *and* for items received between 1 p.m. and 5 p.m., we respond by noon the following business day.

Our community managers and other team members who routinely provide service outside the office use voice mail and email to further enhance and manage expectations. We recommend that they change their personal outgoing voice mail messages daily. These should include warm greetings, summaries of their schedules for the day, when they plan to return phone calls, and how to reach a team member to deal with a time-sensitive matter.

Here is an example of a recommended greeting:

> *Hello, this is Jane Smith, senior community manager with Associa. I'm sorry I missed your call because it's very important to me. I am out of the office today but will return your call upon my return on Tuesday, November 21.*

> *If this is an emergency, please hang up and dial John Doe at 222-222-2222 or press 0 for Customer Service, which will direct your call to John or someone who can assist you. John will take care of your needs in my absence.*
>
> *Thanks for calling Associa!*

This simple practice can lay the foundation for a positive customer interaction. Most important, it manages the expectations of callers so they are not disappointed if their calls are not returned immediately and so they can be available for the return call. This message can save time by eliminating a frustrating cycle of "phone tag." Finally, we offer customers an option for time-sensitive matters that need immediate attention.

Another tool we use to manage expectations is the automatic reply feature or out-of-office message for our emails. This allows the team member to create an automatic reply to incoming email messages. By including the same information recommended for the voice mail greeting, we help the customer set a realistic time frame for a response while also offering options for immediate service needs.

The following example of an out-of-office reply is similar to our voice mail greeting but modified for email delivery:

> *Thank you for your message. I will be on a site visit and away from the office until midafternoon. I plan to return messages this afternoon between 3:30 and 5 p.m. If you need assistance before the end of the day, please contact Sue Scott, sscott@your managementcompany.com, or call 1-800-222-3333.*
>
> *I look forward to connecting with you soon.*
> *Barb Miller*
> *Community Manager*

Our response guidelines provide Associa employees with clear expectations for providing customer service in a manner that we can monitor results. The objectives of our initial responses are to acknowledge customer requests and issues and to begin the process of increasing our understanding of a customer's needs, which then leads to resolving them.

Building Self-Service Tools

We continually focus on building tools to allow our customers to self-serve, therefore handling their needs quickly and efficiently. By giving them the ability to resolve basic issues themselves, our managers need to be involved only when something more complex is needed.

Self-service enables us to satisfy customers at the time, place, and medium in which they seek service. With the smartphone revolution, we have the ability for them to interact with us via our mobile application. They can get self-service twenty-four hours a day, seven days a week, from anywhere in the world.

Social media also is a great medium for self-service. The key is for us to monitor and respond to any request posted on any of its many varieties. Near-immediate responsiveness is needed to satisfy many customers.

While responding quickly is critical, self-service also is about setting expectations for resolution. Timely resolution is dependent on the complexity of the request. This means we must give our customers reasonable timelines regarding when their service requests will be resolved or when they will hear from us regarding next steps.

We use case management via our systems to monitor, drive, and evaluate visibility and accountably in responsiveness and resolution. This helps us not only to manage the types and timelines of requests and their resolutions but also to evaluate our performance against the requests we receive.

The key to our self-service success is meeting our customers where they are and then serving them timely. As Amazon, Apple, Google, and other tech giants disrupt the customer service industry, staying on top of the ways customers interact with service providers is paramount to staying relevant and contemporary.

Listening Actively

Because demonstrating care means we care as much about our customers' problems as they do, a clear understanding of the issue is required. By listening actively, we can ensure our employees obtain all the information required to support and serve the customer. The steps to resolution generally involve reaching out to others who can help resolve the issues at hand, referring the matter to a maintenance technician, or contacting another professional service firm. This requires employees to understand the matter well enough that they can communicate clearly to someone else.

Above all, customers want us to listen and to show that we care as much about their question or issue as they do. Once we've listened and learned about a customer's concern, it is essential that we express or demonstrate our appreciation for its gravity to the customer and that it is equally important to us. We always must remember that no matter how insignificant or irrelevant a problem may seem to us, it is significant and relevant enough for that customer to take the time to contact us for an answer or resolution.

We stress the following essential steps for listening actively:

- Provide the customer with your undivided attention.
- Tune in to words, feelings, and body language (if applicable).
- Ask clarifying questions.
- Take notes, as appropriate.
- Summarize, reframe, or paraphrase what you hear/ understand.

The positive impacts of active listening are noteworthy. When our employees take the time to listen to customers with the intent of understanding their true issues, they are better prepared to develop appropriate resolutions.

Establishing Reasonable Expectations

Establishing reasonable expectations for resolutions is critical to delivering five star customer service. One of the most common causes of frustration for customers is a lack of communication about how, when, and by whom an issue will be addressed. That is why it is important to, first, discuss the customers' needs and agree on desired outcomes and, second, agree on response times.

When unhappy customers agree on these two issues, they often see hope for a resolution. By helping them understand that we want to be of service, that we need a little time to resolve their issues satisfactorily, and that we truly want to exceed their expectations, we can begin the process of nurturing loyal customers—but only if we succeed on their behalf. Keeping our word and following through until customers are satisfied will reflect our appreciation and respect for them. Doing so also will reflect well on us and on Associa.

Managing Conflict

At times we must communicate in a difficult situation or with a customer who is unhappy or dissatisfied. We begin with questions so that we can gather the necessary information, analyze the situation, and apply solutions to the issues at hand.

It is up to us as service professionals, whether we find ourselves in the middle of a conflict or on the side as observers, to help mediate and resolve. We look for alternative solutions, and when we decide on the best one, we work to build consensus and to praise everyone involved. Even if one argument is considered inaccurate, we emphasize that each perspective has merit and that all points of the conversation are important, at least to the persons expressing, promoting, or defending them.

Time-tested tools for managing conflict include the following:

- Compromising and accommodating opposing sides as much as possible
- Splitting the difference, whether relative to time or money
- Motivating one side to accept the offering of the other side
- Buying time by postponing the decision and garnering more resources to work out an acceptable solution
- Working out a win-win resolution so that each side gets something it wanted
- Reminding all involved that those who adopt an "all or nothing" mentality sometimes get nothing

Using Varied Channels of Communication

At Associa we emphasize the importance of using all available channels of communication and of employing those preferred by our clients and customers. Our priority is to respond via the channel selected by a customer, rather than via our preferences. In other words, we respond by calling those who left voice mails for us, sending text messages and emails to those who initiated such exchanges, and mailing letters to those who wrote to us.

Our employees are free to use their best judgment, however, and to decide whether they will surprise and satisfy a customer more quickly by responding through a different communication channel. Calling someone who sent a letter, for example, can be rewarding, as can calling someone whose problem has not been resolved via three or more email exchanges.

To ensure that using a different channel does not annoy or inconvenience a customer, it may be best to ask permission to do so. If someone emails, for example, a manager could respond by email, writing simply, "May I call you at your convenience to discuss this matter?" Doing so will preclude a problem such as calling someone who emailed, only to learn that he or she has a hearing disability and cannot communicate by telephone. Situations like these remind me of the benefit of our Platinum Rule over the Golden Rule: Treat others the way *they* want to be treated, rather than how *we* would like to be treated.

Developing Written Communication Skills

Through Associa University we develop courses targeted not only for board members and homeowners but also for community managers, service technicians, and other employees. These courses help our team hone their written and oral communication skills.

To make it easy for every member to create effective written communications, we suggest using a four-step process:

1. Define the purpose of your message and ask questions such as, "What is your goal with this communication? Is it to inform, to persuade the reader to take action, etc.?" Be succinct and as informative or persuasive as appropriate.

2. Define your audience and identify what information your audience needs to understand your message.

3. Organize the information you need to include. This is simply the Who, What, Where, When, and How—and sometimes the Why—of the subject.

4. Create the draft, and then revise it to ensure your message is clear, concise, written in a positive tone, and suitable for your reader.

We endorse using this model for all written notices, even email. It precludes the costly mistake of sending a rushed response to a customer, only to omit important details. Following this four-step process will facilitate achieving the desired results, beginning with creating the right response for the customer and providing all essential information.

• • •

Communicating effectively is emphasized in our educational programs for our Associa employees, whether face-to-face, at private or public meetings, by means of reports or other documents, during telephone conversations, by regular mail or email, via technology such as social media and online meetings, or any other means. Our focus always is on learning how to develop written and oral messages that are targeted for specific readers and listeners in such a way to achieve understanding and avoid miscommunication.

SERVICE IN ACTION

Usually our communication occurs as part of the normal course of doing business. Sometimes, however, we must provide excellent communication in the midst of perceived chaos within our communities. This is not easy. Accordingly, imagine my pleasure in receiving the following letter from grateful board members in southern California whose maintenance technician maintained constant and professional communication with them throughout a stressful situation:

> *We want to express our appreciation and gratitude in working so swiftly with us toward repairing and restoring our community due to multiple water leaks and damage we had after a recent damaging storm. After four weeks of continued water leaks, ripped-out walls,*

and much emotional stress, mess, and inconvenience, it was deeply appreciated. Associa responded immediately and targeted the resolution of the issues at hand.

Your lead technician was incredibly helpful and genuinely comforting in communicating to us to stay calm throughout a very stressful situation that continued to grow one drippy leak after another. He was professionally proactive on every level and he kept us informed along the way as to how he handled the restoration and repairs to our condo building.

He made extra effort to ensure that our community could return to some sort of normalcy quickly and gave us daily updates on his progress. That is the marking of not only a professional, but a thoughtful and considerate individual who went above and beyond a job description. He demonstrated character qualities of common courtesy and respect while keeping us constantly informed and calm.

QUESTIONS TO CONSIDER

1. How do you analyze and adapt to your audience and occasion in developing your message and selecting your communication channels?

2. Why should you invest as much in listening to a message as you do in delivering one?

3. Why are office employees and service technicians held to high standards of communication, including appropriate body language and listening skills?

CHAPTER 16

Leading within Our Communities

Leadership is action, not position.

—DONALD H. MCGANNON,
Broadcasting Executive

Leadership truly is a matter of action—demonstrating abilities, loyalty, ethics, and vision. My hope is that everyone who works at Associa, from the mailroom to the executive suite, wants to be a leader by providing five star customer service to our customers and to each other. Anyone who believes himself or herself to be a leader based on only a title or position likely will face frustration and failure within our culture.

I believe that little things matter most. While some consider acts of leadership to be grand or heroic, we take equal pride in our employees who demonstrate leadership by serving our customers on a daily basis. Though their many acts sometimes may seem to go unrecognized, those without leadership titles often are the true heroes of our impressive success.

EXERCISING LEADERSHIP

Exercising leadership begins with professionalism. Our clients hire us to reflect them, and we must keep this understanding at the forefront as we consider both our appearance and our actions. We must work with our clients to create credibility through our knowledge and our ability to guide them in the right direction.

Our goal is to reflect the following characteristics so that our boards are fully confident in our ability to serve them well:

- ♦ Capability: We must be fully capable to perform the requirements of our role.
- ♦ Credibility: We must have knowledge of all aspects of community management and communicate that knowledge effectively.
- ♦ Reliability: We must be available and responsive to the needs of our boards and our communities so they can count on us.
- ♦ Respect: We are respectful at all times and behave in a way to deserve that respect.
- ♦ Image: We must project a professional image and be a strong representation of Associa and of that community.

The following letter from a board president expresses gratitude for a manager who reflects all these characteristics and more. We are proud that he is part of our Associa family:

> *I have had the pleasure of working with Keith in his role as the community manager for one of the most demanding communities of which I have been a part. He is clearly one of the hardest working and most dedicated community managers I have ever known. That is saying a lot, as I have served as a board member for multiple communities for the last six years.*
>
> *Keith has added to the property's value by spearheading the integration of additional features, including a time-intensive and expensive pool renovation project, added security features including a well-trained security force and surveillance camera system,*

landscaping improvements with a much-needed revamp of the property's irrigation system and aesthetic character-defining features, and continual review and maintenance of parking enforcement procedures.

His responsiveness to community concerns and anticipation of possible issues coupled with his business acumen have afforded him the respect of our board, property vendors, as well as great assurance that he will remain our community manager for years to come.

Exercised daily, such leadership results in not only respect and appreciation but also deep loyalty and strong relationships.

DEMONSTRATING LEADERSHIP

We demonstrate leadership for the communities we manage through our role as a trusted advisor. This begins by having a thorough knowledge and understanding of our products and services and how our customers can use them to their advantage. Many of our branches, for example, utilize our web-based accounting portals that provide our board members with access to information 24/7/365. Ensuring that our clients are educated about the portals and understand their benefit is one way we add value. We also offer property maintenance services that can reduce the challenges that arise in caring for the common area. Guiding a client through all these options is another way we display our expertise.

Managing community associations means rarely experiencing the same day twice. Each day is filled with new challenges and offers a need to solve new problems. Our team demonstrates leadership by assisting each board in evaluating problems and resolving its core issues, rather than merely treating symptoms. Once the core issue is resolved, we use our network of specialists to develop options and recommend solutions that consider the specific needs and budget for an individual community.

Some of the issues community associations encounter are complex in nature and difficult to resolve. In these instances, we work quickly to determine the most effective way to escalate the matter to the most appropriate professional. A difficult repair may require the advice of a mechanical engineer, or a dispute between neighbors may call for legal advice. Our goal is to demonstrate leadership by recommending this escalation, even if the client may resist the cost of the needed expertise.

LEADING THROUGH MEETING MANAGEMENT

In the world of community management, we have meetings, lots of them, and at Associa we educate our managers to excel in facilitating their meetings' success. We demonstrate leadership by keeping these meetings within the allotted time and ensuring they are successful. Our meeting philosophy and standardized meeting tools ensure that each meeting is planned carefully and conducted efficiently and respectfully. This starts with creating the agenda, identifying business action items, producing a professional management report with specific recommendations based on our professional experience, and concluding with a detailed package documenting the results of the meeting.

We believe that the purpose of the meeting is for the board of directors to make the decisions necessary to operate the community. Meeting materials are carefully created and packaged with this end in mind. The result is a positive and productive meeting for the board.

Here's one example of how our manager led the way with his community by ensuring a recent board meeting was successful and ended with a clear result:

> *One of Eric's boards was dealing with a serious matter of failing water heaters. Prior to the quarterly meeting, Eric researched the community's financials and budget, contacted local service providers,*

and worked to provide information ahead of time so that the board could come to the meeting prepared to make an educated decision.

At the meeting, he presented a clear plan of action to the board, which they described as "a clear path to a viable solution." Eric moved the board to a quick decision, which saved them unnecessary maintenance expenses and additional headaches.

LEADERSHIP IN DIFFICULT SITUATIONS

While our employees display leadership daily as they interact with their communities, leadership at Associa also is about going above and beyond. There are countless examples of our employees who have demonstrated courage, tenacity, resourcefulness, and quick thinking to exceed the expectations of our customers and coworkers. It is my privilege to share two that illustrate our leadership capabilities and our commitment to serving our clients with five star customer service:

♦ One of our managers in Minnesota was on call for any emergencies that happened over the weekend. Sure enough, she received an emergency call informing her that the air conditioning unit in a clubhouse had stopped working. She contacted vendors on behalf of the board to begin fixing the problem, and they discovered that an extremely dirty filter had caused the coil to freeze. When the vendor turned off the system to allow the unit to thaw and went to purchase a new filter, our manager stayed on the scene until the work was completed and the air conditioner was cooling the clubhouse again. Several residents noticed their community manager was there on a weekend to resolve the air conditioning unit issues and commented that she was doing a great job for them.

- A manager in Raleigh, North Carolina, was about to leave for the day on a hot Friday afternoon in August when she received a call that her community's pool was closed due to shattered glass in the water. She knew many residents would be looking forward to using the pool that weekend, so she worked with the board members and vendors into the evening to get the pool drained, power washed, and refilled. Everything was returned to normal within twenty-four hours, thanks to her help.

By hiring the best personnel and empowering them through education, experience, support, and resources, we are confident that they are prepared to rise to the occasion and to offer stellar customer service, even when they occasionally must sacrifice some weekends so that customers can enjoy theirs.

LEADING THROUGH INNOVATION

Last, I believe one of the most meaningful ways we demonstrate leadership to our clients is through our value of Innovation and Improvement. We continually evaluate the operation of their communities and look for ways to improve the experiences of their members. We listen to our clients and determine how we can serve them better through the addition of new services, new technology, or simply by improving our current processes.

Additionally, we look beyond our industry for how the marketplace and customer service are changing. We know we are not competing only with other management companies but with all service organizations. We must lead the way because our clients' expectations are changing. When board members choose Associa to be their managing agent, I want them to be confident that we are constantly searching for ways to get better each day on their behalf.

Each time we consider a new innovation, we ask ourselves how that change will benefit our clients. Our spirit of innovation has served us well for the almost forty years that we have been in business, and it will continue to do so, as long as our primary reason to innovate remains our focus on client service.

• • •

By exercising and demonstrating our leadership consistently and expertly, we will continue to develop strong relationships with the associations we serve. The result will be mutual respect and loyalty—all part of our customer service.

SERVICE IN ACTION

As a former public servant and longtime resident of Dallas, I am grateful for the bravery of police officers who risk their lives daily to protect our families. Imagine my horror on July 27, 2016, when I learned that a lone assailant killed five Dallas police officers and injured nine others. It was an extremely difficult time for our community, and I remain heartbroken for the families of those who fell in such an unprovoked and unexpected tragedy.

The shootings took place near one of the high-rise communities we manage downtown. During the crisis and afterward, our Associa team members who were in the building made sure everyone was safe and in lockdown mode. As the investigation ensued after the attack and the area was blocked off, our employees helped residents return to their homes safely and as soon as possible. This was an all-night affair for our manager, who did a phenomenal job of showing that in a life-or-death crisis, her top priority was the safety of our residents. Truly, that was heroic leadership and customer service.

QUESTIONS TO CONSIDER

1. If your customer needed help beyond what your contract or commitment required, how would you respond?

2. Regardless of your position, how are you a role model of leadership, and how do you demonstrate this to others?

3. What can you do to ensure that you are continually improving your leadership effectiveness?

CHAPTER 17

Building Relationships

Every great business is built on friendship.

—J. C. PENNEY,

Founder, JCPenney Department Store

Once we establish relationships with our clients, nurturing and strengthening them becomes critical to our success. We do that by treating them as part of our extended Associa family and continuously showing them how much we care. No matter how much we know and how well we perform, our most loyal clients are those who enjoy working with us, like us, and consider us friends. I learned a long time ago that if customers don't like us or enjoy working with us, they won't want to do business with us.

Our Five Star Customer Service Model embraces building relationships as one of our principles because relationships are everything in the service industry. Clients invest their trust in us, an+d we must reward that trust by striving to provide outstanding customer service.

When no effort is made to strengthen and improve relationships, they are more likely to weaken and deteriorate. That is why we strive constantly to improve our relationships with all our customers, no matter their complexity. By doing so we demonstrate our commitment to them and our interest in addressing their needs while helping them protect and enhance their property values.

BUILDING TRUSTING RELATIONSHIPS

Always cognizant that community management is a "people" business, we work with our board members and homeowners to resolve issues, assist them quickly, and provide professional guidance. As part of our Five Star Customer Service Model, we treat everyone respectfully and kindly, no matter what the issue.

We focus equal attention on all our managed communities. Whether clients are easy to satisfy or challenging to please, we believe all are worthy of our service, interest, attention, and care. Rather than concentrating only on attracting new accounts, we also focus on retaining current accounts by building productive relationships with our board clients and their customers.

Although the community association represented by its elected board of directors is our client, we welcome every opportunity to engage with their customers—the homeowners we serve on their behalf. Community managers who keep homeowners happy are more likely to keep board members happy too. What's more, always mindful that today's disgruntled homeowner may be tomorrow's board president, we treat each with the utmost regard.

The way to build relationships in this business is through trust. Boards and homeowners trust that we will perform simple acts like attending monthly and annual meetings; communicating proactively via periodic telephone calls, emails, and newsletters; and being available when our board members or homeowners need us. We also must earn their trust in our expertise and our guidance as we help them benefit from our educational programs and experience. They hire us to deliver information and service that will benefit their customers, and we must demonstrate through our actions that we can help them handle the issues that arise in their communities.

Additionally, our boards must trust us to be there when extraordinary service is needed. These behaviors should be practiced not only by our leaders but also by all members of the Associa team, including our community managers. This could occur when a natural disaster or a fire impacts their community or when a homeowner issue escalates beyond their ability to handle it constructively.

Through the years our strong relationships with clients and customers have served us well. Their loyalty has enabled us to resolve problems caused by our mistakes, empowered us with their trust when we had to address their internal controversies, assisted us by providing favorable references when we sought new clients, and supported us by renewing our contracts.

The following example highlights an employee who built a strong relationship with a customer by going above and beyond to help her in her time of need:

> *Our customer service representative took an upset homeowner and made her very happy with her kindness. The owner received a violation letter for her back porch being out of compliance. When we contacted the owner, she explained that she was ill and on a fixed income.*
>
> *Once she heard that, our employee took time to post on social media that the person was looking for a small table and chairs for her porch, so that she could clean up her porch and bring it into compliance. She was able to find a table and then took it to the owner's home and helped her clean up her porch. She even took a photo with the owner and her Associa book. She absolutely went out of her way to help this owner.*

Managers like this one make me proud. They also underscore the importance of happy employees who go out of their way to make customers happy by assisting them in small but meaningful ways.

MAKING POSITIVE FIRST IMPRESSIONS

Relationships begin with first impressions, which are made in a matter of seconds and never can be undone. At Associa we underscore not only the importance of initial first impressions but also the reality that we may be oblivious to making them. In our business, people are watching everywhere: at the office, at an annual or board meeting, in common areas, in homes, and even in public.

A community manager who stops to pick up trash by the swimming pool, for example, may not realize that he is being observed by a homeowner who happens to be looking out of her window at that time. Such favorable first impressions are bonuses, for those who make them are unaware of the opportunity and come across as sincere, thoughtful, and helpful.

Whenever anyone, anywhere, anytime is aware of us, we are making an impression, regardless of our lack of awareness or unrelated scenario. A manager who wears a strong cologne to meet with a board president who is allergic may create a memorable negative impression, for example. Along similar lines, I chuckled when an employer recently posted online, "The rude driver who took my parking place a few minutes ago and told me to [EXPLETIVE DELETED!] just showed up for his job interview—with me!" You can bet your money that the driver's negative first impression in an unrelated setting certainly impacted his job opportunity.

Every member of our team understands that favorable first impressions are made mainly through our appearance and our communication. By dressing appropriately, using proper language and tone of voice, behaving professionally, and being early or at least punctual for appointments and meetings, we can represent Associa well and put clients at ease.

By comparison, we can make negative first impressions quickly through our appearance, tone of voice, or behavior. Wearing inappropriate attire, using vulgar language, chewing gum in public, or getting intoxicated at receptions certainly can result in bad impressions that weaken relationships and may be difficult to overcome. We are sensitive to the realization that sometimes others observe our behaviors in unrelated social settings outside of the workplace, but these observations can have harmful repercussions. To make matters worse, sometimes strangers observe our employees and may report them to our boards or others.

Through our industry's trade organization, for example, we have many late-night outings and social events. These events are meant to promote networking among community management professionals and local board members. We always must keep in mind that our behavior both on and off the job reflects on our ability to work effectively with those in our communities—regardless of whether they are current clients.

Similarly, positive first impressions made in unrelated settings can be helpful. A new client of ours recently wrote to tell me about the impact of meeting one of our employees at a local grocery store. Neither the employee nor the board member knew then that they would work together one day. Based on their positive interaction long before their business relationship began, however, the board member was confident that she and her community were in good hands.

At Associa we expect great first impressions from everyone, whether a salesperson making a presentation, a manager presenting a report at an annual meeting, a service technician making repairs, a receptionist answering the telephone, or a customer service representative working with a vendor or homeowner. Believe me, first impressions matter.

BECOMING THE RIGHT PARTNER

Our objective with all clients is to be the right partner for them. We do so by guiding them through multiple planning stages to define their vision and goals for their communities. Throughout this process, we work with them to customize a package of services to help them achieve those goals. Then we align expectations and assign a professional community manager to be their primary contact and advocate.

The end result should be a clear road map for the years ahead and a shared understanding of expectations. This attention to our partnership with each client becomes the foundation of our relationship. Central to that relationship, however, is the community manager. Often his or her personalized commitment and service to the community is what makes or breaks the relationship. The example that follows illustrates this principle in action:

> As the community manager for a developing association, Bob volunteered to give up his weekend to be part of the grand opening for their new community clubhouse. As a part of this effort, he trained the on-site team to use the new building systems and stayed on-site for several hours to ensure they knew how to operate everything successfully.
>
> Both the developer and the new board were very pleased by the service he provided to them and the way he helped pull the community together.

Our goal is to convince our clients and customers through our daily actions that we are the right partners for them, especially when the competition offers cheaper alternatives.

ENGAGING THE CUSTOMER

We build relationships with our customers one interaction at a time. We take time with each contact to ensure we record his or her name and contact information correctly, and then we use the customer's name throughout the conversation. We can all relate to our experiences as a customer and how we feel when someone uses our name. It creates an immediate connection between a service provider and a customer.

We ask our Associa family members to be sensitive to how our clients and customers prefer to be addressed. Unlike some companies that train their employees to address customers by first names, we ask ours simply to ask what they prefer. A seventy-year-old homeowner, for example, might prefer to be addressed as "Mrs. Bigley" rather than as "Charlene," while a judge might prefer to be called by her title and surname.

This is an easy way to reflect our respect and consideration for everyone we serve. Such friendly formality and smiling appropriately are effective customer service tools for engaging customers, even during telephone conversations. Generally, a smile communicates that you are happy, likable, and eager to serve; affects your mood positively; and helps your customer enjoy a pleasant experience with you.

Sometimes the nature of our work makes it difficult to engage customers easily. This happens when the legal framework, rules, or guidelines of a community prevent us from fulfilling specific requests. At such times smiling sympathetically may help reflect genuine interest while a community manager struggles to explain the situation fairly, firmly, and politely—with the greatest consideration.

Bothersome pets offer a good example of such situations. A homeowner who cannot sleep because of her neighbor's barking dog may demand that the manager resolve her situation. If the community has no restrictions and the community association has no duty or obligation to provide enforcement procedures for the dog, there is nothing the community manager can do about it. By showing empathy for the customer and searching for alternative solutions, a community manager may be able to engage the customer effectively and create a positive customer service experience, despite the immediate circumstances and its limitations.

SHARING EXPERIENCES

The homeowner who is bothered by her neighbor's barking dog also helps us demonstrate how we can build relationships by sharing experiences. Although we may not always be able to offer a solution to the situation through the association's guidelines, our managers have certainly heard this complaint before and have resources to offer.

One way we do this is by looking for successful outcomes from the past and applying them to the present situation. In this case the community manager can provide the homeowner with contact information for the city's animal control office or community mediation service. He also can provide the homeowner some guidance about how to communicate directly with her neighbor to find a mutually acceptable solution regarding the dog. Our extensive experience sometimes can lead to a satisfied customer, even if we can't provide the solution he or she requested originally.

UNDER PROMISING, OVER DELIVERING

The popular intention to under promise and over deliver is part of Associa's Five Star Customer Service Model. This simple practice involves establishing enough time to complete a request while making every effort to surprise the customer with an earlier-than-promised delivery. It is coupled with our intention of keeping our word by establishing realistic timelines for meeting service requests.

In our business most of the service requests we receive are not emergencies. The most typical are researching a payment made by a homeowner, responding to a routine maintenance request, or gathering information for an upcoming board meeting. They are opportunities for us to promise the requested information on a given time or date and then to try to delight the customer by delivering early.

The benefit of this practice is significant because it creates trust and credibility—two key elements of a strong relationship. Over time these efforts will serve us well when we make a mistake or need extra time to complete a task. In any case, when we communicate a deadline, we must do our best to meet the customer's expectation and then make extra effort to deliver early. Who doesn't love a positive surprise?

APOLOGIZING EARNESTLY

When a customer has had a less than satisfactory experience, he or she deserves an earnest apology. Being sorry is not the same as admitting fault or responsibility for causing a problem. It means connecting with the customer on his or her level; expressing sincere empathy for the situation; and recognizing that if the situation were reversed, we probably would feel exactly the same.

Sincerity is essential, especially because most people can detect phoniness. Apologizing and taking ownership of resolving an issue should help deescalate the situation and facilitate collaborating with the customer to find a solution immediately or based on a mutually acceptable timeline.

I was particularly pleased when a customer took the time to write to me about an employee who offered a sincere apology before resolving a situation. This is a great example of how we build relationships simply by taking ownership of resolving a problem:

> *I just want to let you know your maintenance man took the time today to reprogram my garage door opener again. I have had several problems with it and he has attempted to fix it several times before but with no luck. He apologized that he had not been able to get it to work properly, but I think we were able to finally solve it this time!*
>
> *On a side note, he is always busy working around the complex every time I see him but always takes the time to be helpful. I don't know what all he is scheduled to do, but taking care of six buildings by himself seems to be a heavy load for one person. He has never complained and is always pleasant and courteous to me and to other residents.*

At Associa we regularly assess our customer relationships and learn from both our successful ones and our troubled ones. Above all, we recognize that strong, mutually beneficial relationships are the foundation from which to improve customer service, resolve problems, retain accounts, and get referrals for new accounts. They are the hallmark of our success and an investment in a brighter future.

LEAVING A POSITIVE LAST IMPRESSION

How a customer feels at the end of an interaction is what matters most. When we exceed the expectations of customers with our five star customer service, we typically earn their loyalty.

First impressions may be important, but last impressions generally are the most memorable. These typically are made through small gestures such as friendly farewells; thoughtful statements such as asking, "What else can I do for you?"; and gracious expressions of gratitude for opportunities and business. They are appreciated and usually remembered by the happiest or initially unhappiest of customers.

While we never want to lose a client, how we communicate and behave when we do can determine whether we can earn lost business anew, either now or in the future. Consider this example of how we retained a client because of powerful last impressions:

> *Two of our leaders did not give up on an association that gave us an unexpected letter of termination. The community had been with us for more than ten years and was a very significant client for us.*
>
> *After receiving the termination letter, these leaders went above and beyond and were successful in saving the account. The board president was visiting with the community manager, who brought up some items that we would no longer be handling for the association as a result of the termination. Based on that conversation, the board president began rethinking this recent decision to change management companies.*
>
> *Once we realized the board members might regret their decision, we requested a meeting with the board and were subsequently successful in reversing the board's position.*

As this example illustrates, sometimes making a favorable last impression can reap account benefits. Friendly farewells, favorable last words, and gracious attempts to serve the client at the end are simple but effective ways to make great last impressions.

• • •

At Associa five star customer service begins even before a customer signs on the bottom line and extends consistently throughout the length of a contract. When it's time to renew, we hope our client has an understanding, appreciation, and expectation of the highest level of service. Our way of life is to keep the customer service bar raised high, precluding even a remote possibility that the association could find better service elsewhere.

SERVICE IN ACTION

At times we build relationships because of what might be considered surprising or heroic actions. In these cases the strength and integrity of our employees is what leads to renewed contracts for Associa. I am particularly proud to share an example of a manager in Florida who helped create customer loyalty simply by being himself. Our happy and appreciative homeowner described him as follows:

> I would like to write you about one of your great employees. He was out early this morning loading my truck and somehow my wallet fell out of my pocket. I realized it approximately thirty minutes later. I had over $1000.00 in it, along with several credit cards, my driver's license, etc. I received a call shortly after that from your employee asking me if I lost something. I was so relieved.
>
> There are some great, honest people out there, and your employee is one of them. I offered him a reward and he wouldn't accept anything. I also want to say how he is so involved in this community.

He is outside on all projects and shows me how he cares. He has made a great difference in this community.

QUESTIONS TO CONSIDER

1. How do you establish and nurture strong relationships with your clients and coworkers? Why is this an important aspect of Associa's Five Star Customer Service Model?

2. What level of service do you provide that your customer could not get elsewhere?

3. When you make a mistake or have a customer with a problem, what steps do you take to resolve it?

CHAPTER 18

Owning the Resolution

Accountability breeds response-ability.

—STEPHEN COVEY,
Author and Speaker

Unsurpassed customer service depends on assuming responsibility for resolving a customer's problem and on following up when we need a colleague's assistance to do so. Our standards for integrity and accountability certainly are consistent with our "response-ability," that is, with our having the abilities and resources to respond swiftly to resolve issues for clients and customers.

STEPPING UP TO RESPONSIBILITY

Simply handing off a problem for someone else to handle is unacceptable. Owning the resolution means that the person who first interacted with the customer will either resolve the situation or identify someone else who can—and later will follow up to ensure that the customer is satisfied.

Realizing that most customers want to know that we listen and care as much about their problems or issues as they do, we make every effort to do so. In fact, we welcome every opportunity to use the resources at our disposal to demonstrate our commitment to clients and customers. When our team member who was a customer's initial point of contact reaches out for assistance, for example, he or she must follow up to ensure that the customer's problem was solved.

Following up means contacting the appropriate internal resource—even if he or she works in another department or in another state—as well as the customer. Doing so reflects our accountability and reinforces our ability to listen and to care.

DEMONSTRATING INTEGRITY
AND ACCOUNTABILITY

Any Associa employee who is asked a question, receives a request for information, or needs help resolving an issue regarding a particular community is expected to track down the answer. The question may be about the status of a maintenance request, the date of the next board meeting, or a more complicated matter regarding an assessment account. The answer may be in the form of a procedure, policy in question, or form required to assist the homeowner.

Many requests will require the assistance of another Associa team member. Such instances are excellent opportunities to demonstrate our value of Integrity and Accountability by closing the loop to ensure that the customer received the requested information and is satisfied. Simply transferring the request is not enough; we hold ourselves accountable for following a customer's request to its conclusion.

As with many organizations, we have multiple customer service numbers for our customers to call when they have an issue. Sometimes customers inadvertently choose the wrong number and consequently reach employees at our service center in Texas instead of someone at their local branch office. When this happens, the employees work with their team members in the local market to ensure a warm handoff with the customer. I expect them to work together to ensure the customer's needs are met, regardless of whether they can solve the issue themselves.

BEING RESPONSIVE

Managing a community well means the occasional late night and many interesting situations. Often it means we must own issues caused by homeowners in the communities we manage or be responsible for carrying out the wishes of their boards. Regardless of the situation or who caused a problem, our role is to be responsive. We may not be responsible for creating an issue, but we are accountable for resolving it. This entails dealing effectively in many different situations, including, for example, working with a homeowner who was mistakenly charged for a violation he didn't commit or handling a dispute between a board member and a homeowner.

The diversity of the problems with which our community managers must deal was underscored after a community's annual homeowners' event. The board president contacted me to tell me how impressed he was by our manager's service. While this particular experience is out of the norm, it demonstrates our commitment to own the resolution to every problematic situation that develops under our watch in the communities we manage:

> We were unable to get our water turned on last Saturday evening after our community's annual pig roast; therefore we could not complete the clean-up of the area in front of the outdoor pool entrance.
>
> Our manager heard about this from some of our residents and came over the next morning to clean and straighten up the area. We were so appreciative of his service; it truly is an example of going above and beyond. We are grateful for the many things he does for our community. He wears many hats and never complains.

RESOLVING DIFFICULT SITUATIONS

Owning the resolution becomes particularly important when we are dealing with a difficult customer or a situation beyond our direct control. Failure to close the loop can make these situations even more challenging and can escalate the emotion involved. When dealing with a difficult client, we must go back to the basics, which starts with active listening, clearly understanding the issue at hand, coming to agreement on the solution, and agreeing on a time frame for resolving the matter in question.

At times we encounter problems that seem unsolvable. In such instances we cannot allow the problem to paralyze us and must look for new solutions or involve external resources for assistance. If we continue to act quickly and involve other Associa team members and leaders, we likely will find a solution that meets the customer's needs.

Working quickly through this process can be key to avoiding an escalation that could be costly for our clients. One example of this occurred when we had an internal issue with a telephone installation, which resulted in hundreds of customer calls going unanswered. Our team quickly jumped in to remedy the situation and calmed the unhappy customers. Its success was recognized in the following message I received from one of our leaders:

> Kristine and her team demonstrated responsiveness and attentiveness by returning hundreds of calls and emails which were misplaced as a result of a recent telephone upgrade.
>
> They efficiently handled this curve ball with patience and maintained a calming presence while calling our clients and vendors back and responding to their requests. All of the members of this team consistently maintain a positive attitude while encouraging each other, and this attitude gets translated to our clients on a daily basis. The team supports one another and is an example of family spirit at its best.

• • •

To demonstrate our exceptional level of care, we must exert great effort to ensure customers' issues are resolved. It takes ownership and a true can-do attitude to own something we did not create and then to continue through the resolution until the customer is satisfied.

SERVICE IN ACTION

In our business, we must find solutions to issues we did not cause but that create hurdles for our clients. This can involve community meetings where decisions must be made to move an issue forward. Here is an example set by one of our employees in Virginia who went above and beyond to own a resolution for one of our boards:

> Last month, there was an annual meeting scheduled for a client whose manager was out on vacation. The board was five ballots short of reaching quorum. One of our administrative assistants called from the post office to say there were five ballots that had come in the mail that afternoon. Unfortunately, no one at the office could take them to the meeting due to other commitments.
>
> Without hesitation, this administrative assistant obtained the address of the meeting from her supervisor and showed up at the meeting location much to the board's surprise with the five ballots they needed to approve the vote. It was the first time this client reached quorum in many years. Needless to say they were impressed with all of the resources Associa has to serve them. We are very proud to have this administrative assistant as a part of our team.

QUESTIONS TO CONSIDER

1. What are ways you can own the resolution for your customers?

2. How do you use your resources to ensure the customer's issue is solved?

3. How do you follow up with a customer to gauge his or her satisfaction with the resolution?

CHAPTER 19

Giving Back to Our Community at Large

Only a life lived in the service to others is worth living.

—ALBERT EINSTEIN

The associations we manage do not live in isolation but, rather, within the larger geographic communities beyond their boundaries. That is why our five star customer service simply is not complete without our also serving and giving back to the community at large. This practice is especially important for us, given that our industry serves communities.

SERVICE TO OTHERS

I have found that our employees strive for better service when they are engaged and understand that their jobs relate to a greater purpose, that is, in service to others. Such a purpose elevates our role above delivering on the lifestyle and vision of the board members and homeowners who live in the communities we serve. This is the greater purpose that weds Associa's community management and corporate citizenship together and extends our Five Star Customer Service Model to true community service.

Today both employees and clients want to see and feel that service providers care about more than profits. They want the companies they hire, seek to hire, or seek to be hired by to have a greater purpose and mission. Our agreement with that perspective is reflected in Associa's Corporate Citizenship Programs, including Associa Supports Kids, Associa Green, and Associa Cares. We also participate in numerous national and local partnerships that help create the programs that serve our communities and even those we don't serve. Cumulatively, they afford us many rewarding opportunities to make a difference.

HOW ASSOCIA GIVES BACK

Our ability to deliver additional services to our customers demonstrates our leadership to our communities and within the community management industry. To give back to our customers' communities and to our society at large, Associa has developed several unique community service programs. No other company in our industry sponsors such programs or devotes this level of financial and human resources in promoting community service. Additionally, we coordinate and plan events around popular holidays and support local children's sports leagues. In essence, we help create the lifestyle that our communities envision.

Associa family members particularly enjoy participating in our community outreach programs. Our best-known and most successful community service programs include Associa Supports Kids (ASK), Associa Green, and Associa Cares, which are described briefly below:

Associa Supports Kids

Through Associa Supports Kids we promote healthy and enriching activities for children in our client communities. We do this in a wide variety of ways, including the following:

- Attending community events with our Associa mascot, Scout the golden retriever, to distribute information about keeping children safe and active.

- Sponsoring organized youth activities in which a child living in an Associa-managed community participates. Our goal is to benefit the whole group, whether it is a sports, art, or academic activity.

- Participating in child-focused events, such as Read Across America. Every year our executive team celebrates this occasion on behalf of Associa Supports Kids by reading to children in local schools.

Additionally, because Associa Supports Kids is so focused on safety, we're a national sponsor of the National Association of Town Watch (NATW) National Night Out events, an effort that helps forge community-police partnerships in our client communities as well as in other communities across the country. This program promotes getting neighbors out to meet one another and to engage with local law enforcement and first responders—when they are not needed—to help make our communities safer for children and families.

Associa's outreach includes sharing ASK materials, such as Scout's Safety Tip coloring and activity books, ChildPrint ID kits, and "Safe & Strong" silicone wristbands, with participating Associa- and non-Associa-managed communities. To help support these gatherings, Scout attends when and where available, and each year the number of communities that contacts us for support grows by 15–25 percent.

Associa Green

Our Associa Green program fosters environmentally friendly practices in community associations by supporting, promoting, and helping communities achieve green initiatives. We fulfill this goal in several ways, including the following:

- When invited by communities, we attend events and distribute information about sustainable living. Some of them have separate green committees that host events entirely focused on environmental initiatives in which we are proud to participate, such as Earth Day and other special occasions.

- We bestow the Associa Green Award to Associa-managed communities that employ innovative ways to be better stewards of the environment. Given annually, this honor recognizes efforts to promote green living through strategies such as LED lighting upgrades, shredding and recycling events, storm water management, and even using goats to remove invasive weeds.

- If a community expresses interest in "going green," Associa Advantage recommends vendors that offer environmentally friendly services and products.

Associa Green is based on the belief that "living green" creates a better life for our communities and for our planet, and we are committed to working alongside our boards and homeowners to pursue this worthy ideal.

Associa Cares

Truly one of our company's great success stories, Associa Cares is our corporate charity that provides financial assistance to families whose homes have been affected by natural or man-made disasters, regardless of whether they live in an Associa-managed community.

Through it we provide monetary donations to families with impacted homes in any community, regardless of whether we manage it. While this occasionally happens when an individual reaches out to us, more often our branches refer residents in associations they manage or people they know in the larger community who have suffered a flood, fire, earthquake, tornado, hurricane, landslide, or other disaster.

From its inception to the time of this writing, Associa Cares has raised more than $5 million in disaster relief to assist more than two thousand families. This accomplishment has been possible only because of the generous donations of our employees and partners. Our branches and staff have implemented several creative ways to raise this money, including the following:

- Fund-raisers. Associa's home office recently hosted a chili cook-off, with all the proceeds from the admission price donated to Associa Cares. Events like this also demonstrate our commitment to family spirit.

- Payroll deductions. Many of our employees generously elect to voluntarily give Associa Cares an amount of their choosing from every paycheck.

- Branch events. Many of our branches host golf tournaments and vendor speed dating events that allow community managers and vendors to connect while raising money for families in crisis.

We're proud of how dedicated our employees are to this cause and to the others we support through Associa Supports Kids and Associa Green. It's one of the key ways we ensure the value of community continues to serve people everywhere.

• • •

Driving a culture of service without having a culture of giving back is extremely difficult. I am excited about what lies ahead for us as a company, but I also am aware that only by providing excellent service every day are we likely to realize that future. My challenge as CEO, and my challenge to Associa, is to continue to focus on tomorrow while serving our clients and customers today and connecting our employees and clients to the greater purpose of giving back.

SERVICE IN ACTION

Early in the spring of 2017 a fire destroyed four units in one of our Florida communities. The families who lived in those units lost everything, and our local branch understandably wanted to help. They referred the residents to Associa Cares.

Because one of the employees of the branch lived only a few miles from the community in which this devastating fire took place, she asked if she could deliver the checks to the impacted families. She later sent us this note detailing her gratitude for everything Associa does through our charitable work:

> *I can't put into words how proud it made me to know that we, Associa, care about our residents. I cried after leaving the first lady, a single mother of two who lost everything. She was so grateful, and you could tell what a difference this was going to make for her and her family. So, thank you! Thank you so very much for being here and helping people in need. I am so proud to work for Associa!*

QUESTIONS TO CONSIDER

1. What types of corporate citizenship programs does your company have?

2. How does your company encourage employees to give back for the greater good?

3. What skills and resources from your industry can you use to give back?

PART V

DEALING WITH SHORTCOMINGS IN SERVICE

DEALING WITH SHORTCOMINGS IN SERVICE

Customers don't expect you to be perfect. They do
expect you to fix things when they go wrong.

—DONALD PORTER,
Vice President, British Airways

INTRODUCTION

By practicing the elements of our Five Star Customer Service Model,
we strive to deliver perfect service. Realistically, however, that is impossible for any business, including ours, regardless of how hard we try. What
is important is that we try our best and recover quickly when things go
wrong. Failing to address a client's or a customer's concern is inexcus-
able, and following through to ensure resolution is our top priority.

In our business model we customize services for each community, and what might look like a service failure actually can be the
correct execution of our contract. This means the first thing we must
do is assess a problematic situation and determine if a service failure
occurred. If it did and we are at fault, our goal is to satisfy the upset
customer within the boundaries we have, knowing that if we recover
well, we are likely to keep that client.

We must keep all these facets in mind when we find ourselves in a situation in which we need to recover from a service failure. Most important, we must keep our customers in mind and do what we can to help them understand the situation and be satisfied with the end result.

The three chapters that compose Part V focus on how the structure of our service model impacts our ability to recover when we fail. Our framework includes specific steps that our employees follow as they deal with shortcomings related to failure or to change.

CHAPTER 20

Stepping toward
Customer Service Recovery

The customer is not always right, but he
always has the right to be treated right.

—MYRON S. STA. ANA,
Training Consultant

Our road to service recovery begins with an understanding of the housing segment we serve, namely, community associations.

Community associations are fairly new legal entities. They embody modern property ownership principles that use contract law and property, or deed, restrictions that govern the rights and behaviors intended to preserve the community as a whole. These deed restrictions also are referred to as covenants.

Typically these covenants create standards for maintaining common and personal property in a manner that enhances property values. In fact, according to the American Enterprise Institute, the common property combined with the rules of a community association help homes in a community association demand a price premium of from 5 to 10 percent higher than in a traditional community that has no community association. Supporting the common amenities and the covenants that require enforcement, however, can create a customer service challenge.

The result of this structure is that our customer relationship is different from other service providers because we must serve two groups, each with different expectations. Our primary relationship is with the board of directors who engages us to maintain the common property and provide the administration of the community. We also serve the homeowners or members by administering the services provided by the community on behalf of the board. Therefore, we always must bear in mind that the members of the community are our customers as well, second only to the board.

Often these relationships lead to conflict or to service issues that are the outcome of our proper execution of a policy or directive of the board of directors that might not be to the liking of a homeowner. In such cases the customer may not have a clear understanding of the policy or of our role in resolving the matter. Either way, we must treat him or her with the utmost respect and try to be of assistance in any way possible. Inevitably, however, such circumstances can complicate our ability to identify and resolve service issues.

CUSTOMER SERVICE RECOVERY

When a concerned or upset customer contacts us, our procedure is to go beyond simply determining who is right or wrong. This process is our definition of and what we call service recovery. Responding appropriately begins with understanding our role in resolving the situation, the responsibilities defined in our contract to the community, and the origin of the underlying issue, and must be done while interacting with the customer with the greatest professionalism, courtesy, consideration, and respect. Looking at essential factors can help us determine the level of effort required and the direction the manager or the customer needs to pursue to resolve the issue. These factors include the following:

- The issue that needs to be resolved
- The customer's desired outcome
- The source of the issue
- The party or parties who can provide a resolution
- Associa's responsibility in finding an effective solution.

These and other factors impact our role and our required steps in solving the problem. Often it's not a step-by-step approach, especially given the complexities of our multiple relationships. Nevertheless, we offer our managers a framework of the best way to proceed:

Assess the Issue

Step one in identifying the problem is to assess the underlying issue and understand the situation or complaint. The best way to do this is simply to listen to the customer without interrupting. Once the customer is finished, we confirm our understanding by asking clarifying questions and restating the problem back to the customer.

Define the Customer's Desired Outcome

As the underlying issue becomes clearer, we should ask the customer what he or she would like to see as a resolution to the situation. This does not mean that we have to agree with that desired outcome, especially if it is unreasonable, but it does provide us the ability to understand the customer's expectation for the issue at hand. To work toward that goal, we listen, empathize, articulate the desired outcome back to the customer, and provide a target deadline for following up if the issue cannot be resolved during the call or meeting.

Uncover the Source of the Problem

Once the customer's issue and desired outcomes are understood clearly, the next step is to uncover the source of the underlying problem. This means determining whether the issue was triggered by an action or inaction by Associa, by the board, or by a service provider or whether it is based on a dispute with neighbors or other persons. To respond appropriately requires understanding how the issue was generated.

We applied these steps for recovery, for example, in a specific situation in which our community manager made a significant mistake regarding a large community project. By assessing the issue, defining the customer's desired outcome, and uncovering the source of the problem, we were able to put the project back on track and repair our relationship with the board.

Good intentions can sometimes lead to bad experiences, and this was the case for our community manager in Nevada. After many years of experience managing shopping centers, he developed an interest in community associations and accepted a position as a community manager. His transition went smoothly due to his understanding of site management and maintenance as he oversaw many projects in his previous role. One of the large single-family home communities in his portfolio was preparing to do some road replacement and resealing. He had a solid relationship with the board of directors of this community, and they had utmost confidence in his abilities. As the planning for the road project began, the community manager shared his experience with shopping center parking lots and also offered to provide introductions to some of the contractors with whom he had worked in paving projects.

The board responded by moving the project management duties of the asphalt project to the community manager and decided not to engage the engineering firm that had supervised previous projects. Because he enjoyed project management work, the community manager was happy for the opportunity to support the community in this way. He did not consult his branch leaders before accepting this assignment.

The early phases of the project went smoothly. He requested and received three road replacement proposals from contractors with whom he had worked previously, and the board approved one quickly. The project began on schedule.

On the first day of diverting traffic for the repairs, however, the problems began first thing in the morning. As traffic backed up at the exit gates and blocked other roadways, homeowners became frustrated and angry because they would be late for work and/or their children would be late for class. Phones at the management company office and at board members' homes rang off the hook.

Apparently the community manager and contractor missed some important details during the project planning. Paving experts know that one of the challenges during a road replacement project is diverting traffic during each phase and communicating regularly and effectively with homeowners so that they know which entrances are open and closed before they leave their homes in the morning. Shopping center parking lots, by comparison, do not require this level of planning because the paving usually can be completed by restricting access to certain parts of the lot over the course of the project, leaving other areas open for patrons.

The project had to be stopped and postponed to allow for the engagement of the engineer, the development of a new plan, and proper notification to the owners.

This delay cost the contractor his performance bonus, cost the manager his solid reputation, and potentially cost Associa a client.

What went wrong? In this case, the community manager simply forgot to follow his own advice and rely on experts. While many experiences are transferable to community management, many are not. Our community manager was excited about managing the project and did not take the time to think through all the requirements. If the engineering firm had been contacted, the traffic planning and notification process would have been at the top of the list. Unfortunately, a solid reputation can be tarnished with one mistake, and a lack of confidence created in one action.

The solution. Fortunately, there were no financial consequences to the association for the poor planning and communication. There were, however, consequences for the manager, as the client had lost faith and confidence in his abilities. Associa assigned a new community manager to the account and increased supervision for a substantial period. The experience was a solid reminder of why the primary role of a community manager is to provide guidance and recommend the experts that communities need to operate smoothly.

Identify Agents of Resolution

Identifying the source of the problem is essential to identifying the person or persons who have ownership of any potential solution. If a homeowner is upset about a board's decision, the problem can be resolved only by the board—and certainly not by us acting in isolation or without the board's input.

This is an important point. While we always strive to own the resolution, this does not mean we are able to solve all problems, especially if we were acting appropriately on the board's behalf. While perception may seem to be reality for that upset homeowner, what looks like a service issue may actually reflect our proper execution of the association's policy or a board's decision.

Gauge Associa's Responsibility in Recovery

Because our community managers are the point of contact for communities and their boards, too often there is a misperception that we are solely responsible for resolving disputes and that we are paid highly to perform that duty. Many of our customers wrongly believe that the entirety of the association assessments they remit to us for processing are our management fee. The truth is that the percentage of a homeowner's assessment that is applicable to our management fee generally is less than 5 percent of the total. Nevertheless, this misconception is difficult to correct.

When a complaint involves action undertaken by the board, such as a decision to levy a fine for a covenant violation, we may have to handle misdirected anger. Often part of our service recovery is to educate homeowners about the roles and responsibilities of all parties involved and the policies in the community. Creating a common understanding of these roles and clearing misconceptions may help resolve an issue but will not necessarily realize the customer's desired outcome.

Once the issues and relevant parties have been identified, finding true resolution to the problem can be the more difficult challenge. This is in part driven by the popular notion that the "customer is always right" and that as a service company we must do everything and anything possible to please the customer. That may be a romantic notion of how things work, but ultimately it is unsustainable. Five star customer service requires a response that is appropriate for the situation, is delivered honestly, and leads to the best solution possible under the community's governing documents and our contractual guidelines.

When issues arise from Associa's management practices, escalating the response is fairly clear. When they arise from board action, by comparison, resolution requires engaging parties outside the Associa family. If the board, for example, levies a special assessment to complete an important restoration project, an upset homeowner may call to complain. In this case, however, the complaint is in response to a board action, and the board is the only party who can determine whether reconsideration is possible.

In such cases, after listening to the customer and understanding the issue, the manager should explain how and why the board made the decision. The next step would be to offer to arrange a discussion with the board president or to provide information about the next regular board meeting. Because the power to resolve the issue is in the hands of the elected board, our appropriate response is to hear the problem, explain the role of the board, and offer to facilitate communication or meetings between the board and the aggrieved party.

Similarly, customer dissatisfaction may arise from disputes between other residents within the community. Serving the customer in this situation can become challenging. As with any customer issue, listening and assessing the issue and desired solution is the first step. If the dispute relates to rules governing the community, then it would be appropriate for us to enforce the policy as written. If the dispute involves an issue that is not related to the rules governing the community and is more related to interpersonal conflict, then it is appropriate to explain the scope of the authority of the board and manager and note that the community does not have the authority to solve the issue. In some states there are state-sponsored mediation programs that provide a forum to resolve disputes. In such cases it may be appropriate to direct the customer to these resources.

These types of issues may be clouded by emotions or threats of litigation. When this happens, it is appropriate to focus on what makes Associa unique. Our resources and scope of services allow us to provide expertise for responding to conflict effectively. Our legal, marketing, and external affairs employees in our home office stand ready to help all employees assess the best course of action and the appropriate scaled response to any challenge. This family spirit not only makes us unique but also puts us in the best position to scale our five star customer service responses appropriately.

• • •

Going into denial when things go wrong is unacceptable at Associa. Our immediate goal always is to determine what happened, why, what can be done about it, when, and by whom. Taking responsibility for addressing issues at hand begins with listening, learning, and responding while interacting constructively with everyone involved. By having defined steps for our employees to follow in customer service recovery, we enhance our ability to make things right as quickly and satisfactorily as possible. Our goal is to transform any unhappy customer into an even more loyal one by resolving problems efficiently and effectively.

SERVICE IN ACTION

Our team was required to gauge Associa's responsibility in response to an issue that involved both the association board and its community manager. While it appeared on the surface that the community manager simply was executing the board's directives—a situation in which we wouldn't be at fault—the truth was that the board's actions were not in line with the governing documents. Because our community manager should have been familiar enough with the financials and governing documents of the association to know that the board's directives violated the association's covenants, this service error was our mistake. By applying our customer service recovery steps to this situation, however, we were able to correct course and keep the client.

Several years ago we began managing a large community in California. The board of directors were members who had been elected and reelected for years and therefore had served for a long time. As a result they were quite active in the day-to-day running of the community and had strong opinions about how the operations were performed.

Our community manager had been with the company for almost a year and was eager to begin managing this new client. She jumped into the role enthusiastically, working hard to build the new relationship. During the first few months, she focused on resolving homeowner complaints, following board directives, and completing items on the action item list. She trusted the board's understanding of the operation and so did not read the governing documents or the management agreement. Some of the action items she completed involved contracting for the replacement of fences and patio railings on the property.

Also during the course of that first year, a group of homeowners became concerned about the board's spending of association funds. The annual meeting was approaching, and this group nominated new candidates for seats on the board of directors. When the election was held, the new candidates won, and new directors had a majority on the board. These new directors took a methodical approach to governing and began their tenure by thoroughly reviewing the governing documents and analyzing the decisions made by their predecessors and actions taken by management.

The new board presented our branch office a sixty-day notice to improve or face nonrenewal of our management agreement. Some of the concerns they presented to support this action are listed below:

- The fence and railing project approved by the previous board was actually for maintenance of exclusive-use common areas, which were the owner's responsibility to maintain.

- Site inspections were not occurring as scheduled in the management agreement. (The manager was relying on the previous board to complete site inspections and to turn over required actions to the manager.)

- A lack of confidence in our competence and ability to deliver services.

In an attempt to make the client happy, the community manager had immediately focused on accomplishing tasks instead of on reviewing the governing documents, financial reports, and common area details before making thoughtful recommendations to the board. In addition to not completing this review initially, she wrongly assumed that the board members understood the governing documents thoroughly, and she did not question their actions.

The first step toward the solution was to acknowledge the mistake and take concrete actions to prevent it from happening in the future. In this circumstance, the local branch leaders got involved to support and ensure better communication with the board and to monitor our progress on the resolutions. The manager was coached to thoroughly review the documents and develop a plan for operating the community over the next year. The branch leader supported the service improvements by aligning the board's expectations with our responsibilities and continued to have regular conversations with the board president to assess our efforts. As a result, we achieved positive outcomes and kept the client.

QUESTIONS TO CONSIDER

1. What complexities in your environment complicate service recovery?

2. How do you work with multiple parties to resolve a complaint?

3. How can you better educate your customer about your role in solving issues for them?

CHAPTER 21

Recovering from Service Failures

Your most unhappy customers are
your greatest source of learning.

—BILL GATES,
Founder of Microsoft

Most people understand the concept that no one is perfect and that we all make mistakes. When we do, generally even the most critical customers can be understanding. That is why homeowners who reach out to us to help resolve their problems offer the best opportunities to demonstrate our commitment to customer service. In fact, properly handling a service failure is the best way to connect with clients and customers and to build long-lasting, positive relationships. What is important is that we learn from the process and that we endeavor to ensure that problems do not reoccur.

Five star customer service doesn't mean being error free. It means fixing our mistakes immediately and completely. If a customer is unhappy, we must expedite our efforts to identify the cause of the problem and to resolve it on the spot. Whatever the occasional customer service error may be, our goal is to recover the customer's goodwill, strengthen the relationship—and keep the customer.

Unfortunately, many customers who are unhappy do not take the time to complain. It is our responsibility to them and to those who do contact us with an issue to listen and to make systematic changes where necessary to prevent service failures in the future.

CORRECTING MISTAKES

While no one likes admitting to a mistake, resolving an issue with a customer is easiest when our action or inaction is the source of the underlying issue. From time to time a keystroke error, an old address, or another small oversight can create an issue for our clients. A good example is a mailing error in which the wrong homeowner received a past due notice. Similarly, an error from our accounting team could cause a unit owner to receive a past due assessment notice, when in fact, payments are current. Similarly, a violation notice could be sent on the same day that the alleged violation was corrected.

In these types of situations, resolving the issue is easier because both the source and solution of the issue fall solely under our authority to correct. In this case, our goal is to listen to the customer, explain and sincerely apologize for the error, and do our best to remedy the mistake instantly. Often an appropriate apology, perhaps followed by a thoughtful goodwill gesture, will resolve the complaint.

Every business and industry has experience in dealing with customers who are dissatisfied with service recovery when things go wrong. Studies show that unhappy customers look for the following responses:

- Appropriate compensation for the failure ("Appropriate" is perceived by the customer)
- Ability of the employee originally contacted to solve the issue and be empowered to make the change

The expectation of compensation can be resolved by actions such as refunding a payment made in error, offering an apology, issuing a credit for services, or returning to complete a repair. Our customers usually react positively when we give them options to resolve their issues. If they remain unsatisfied, then we realize we failed to meet their expectation and must try harder, so we do.

In addition to knowing that we own the mistake and are sorry for it, customers must know when they can expect the issue to be resolved. If resolution will take more than a day or two, it is important for us to make follow-up calls or send emails to demonstrate care and interest. We also know the importance of solving a customer's issue quickly. Time only exacerbates frustration and conflict, and in a service failure situation, we must react with urgency.

PREPARING EMPLOYEES
FOR SERVICE RECOVERY

Service recovery also ties closely to employee satisfaction. Often in a service recovery issue, our employees are put in a difficult position, that is, the need to resolve an issue they did not create directly. The appropriate employee response includes concern, sincerity, and resolve. We must respond not only with a solution but often also with a need to explain why the failure occurred in the first place.

This is where our skill of owning the resolution becomes even more important, as we must not blame others internally for the failure. We must communicate that at Associa we are a team and that the failure of one person or department is taken seriously by all. Such loyalty is critical because the customer is unlikely to contact the employee who made the mistake. Often an unhappy customer will complain to any and all who will listen—so we begin recovery by listening.

When recovering from a service mistake, we have specific procedures to turn a negative into a positive, an unhappy customer into a happy one. Our goal is to empower our employees to solve the customer issue and to give them flexibility to do so, so that we can have one-call resolution. We tend to follow a well-known and popular framework for problem solving, represented by the acrostic HEAT. It follows:

- **H**ear them out.
- **E**mpathize.
- **A**cknowledge or apologize.
- **T**ake charge (and follow through).

When employees know and use simple tools like these, they can be well equipped to resolve a customer's issue.

LEARNING FROM MISTAKES

When a problem occurs, no matter how small and insignificant or large and painful, we address it head-on. We do our best to identify it clearly and completely and then to analyze its parts and subparts as necessary to resolve it. Even as we implement solutions, we ask ourselves questions such as the following:

- What went wrong—and why?
- How could we have avoided this problem?
- What can we do to prevent it from happening again?
- What else can we do to exceed the customer's expectations?
- How should I follow through to ensure we resolved the root of the problem so it does not occur again?
- What lessons learned can I share with my colleagues?

By asking these questions internally and sharing service failures with others, we can track trends and make larger improvements that help to ensure those issues do not happen again.

As a service business, we know it is more expensive to acquire new customers than to keep current ones. Not resolving small issues today can result in big losses tomorrow. Addressing issues and solving problems to completion are critical to our operations today and in the future. Ignoring or denying them—hoping they just go away—usually guarantees they evolve into more serious matters, which could lead to strained, resentful, and frustrated client relationships.

• • •

Clearly, Associa's five star customer service means solving problems quickly and appropriately while also learning from them. We have learned through experience that our most loyal customers are those whose problems were resolved beyond their expectations. While we hope we do not make many mistakes, we work to ensure that we recover well when we do and therefore create stronger, lasting customer relationships.

SERVICE IN ACTION

We were able to put these principles into practice when one of our community managers failed to maintain communication with an unsatisfied homeowner. By working as a team to recover from the customer service error and equipping our employee to handle similar customer service issues in the future, we turned the situation around and ultimately resolved the customer's—and the community's—issue.

Earlier I explained how our service to the association and the board of directors might at times appear to conflict with our service to a homeowner. This can occur when a complex maintenance and repair issue needs to be resolved. That was the case at a condominium development in Florida.

The development was approximately fifteen years old and was starting to experience water leaks from the tile roof and stucco siding. Initially the board was repairing those leaks one at a time until it became clear that this problem was widespread, requiring a more comprehensive solution. The board hired a construction expert to assess the scope of the repair while looking at the financial requirements of the global repair. During the nine months it took to develop a repair plan, additional homeowners experienced leaks. Although all homeowners received the same information and timeline for their repair, one rather aggressive man continued to call weekly to inquire about the status, often raising his voice and becoming confrontational with our community manager.

The community manager began to avoid the regular call and delay the return response to the owner. Before long, he was no longer upset about the repair but, rather, was upset that our community manager was not responding timely. This was the beginning of a destructive cycle, resulting in a complaint to the board during the open forum portion of the board meeting. Those in attendance, including board members and homeowners, now had the impression that we were not providing acceptable customer service for the members of the community.

In this situation, our community manager was organized, proactive, and results-oriented but uncomfortable with confrontation. He was not consciously avoiding the owner; he was simply focusing on other priorities. After the board contacted our local branch president about the complaint, our first step was to examine the facts to determine what our actual actions had been to the owner's complaints. Our maintenance records clearly indicated that for the first six of the nine months, the homeowner received a quick response to his calls and emails. The decline in the response time after that verified that the appropriate level of customer service was lacking.

We needed to solve two problems. The first was to assure the homeowner that he was not being ignored by the board. To accomplish this goal, we recommended that the construction expert performing the evaluation inspect his unit and determine whether a short-term solution could minimize the inconvenience of the current leak.

The second issue was to provide the community manager with additional tools to help him approach these situations differently. Through coaching and skill development we were able to empower our community manager to handle conflict more effectively going forward.

QUESTIONS TO CONSIDER

1. If you make a mistake that impacts a client, what tools do you employ to recover?

2. How do you help diffuse the customer's emotion and own the resolution?

3. How can you communicate service issues and their resolution internally so that you can ensure they do not happen again?

CHAPTER 22

Serving through Change

Change before you have to.

—JACK WELCH,

Former Chairman and CEO, General Electric

While correcting customer service mistakes might seem like the biggest hurdle to service recovery, serving our customers through times of change is another formidable challenge. Providing five star customer service is a high expectation in everyday business, and during times of upheaval it becomes that much more difficult—and that much more important.

Change takes multiple forms and degrees of magnitude, and understanding the nature of a specific change is the cornerstone of successfully serving clients in their midst. Whether the situation includes an adjustment of policy or procedure, the implementation of a new technology, or a sweeping shift in operations or leadership, we can minimize the pain of change for our customers and employees if we anticipate its various ripple effects and plan to address them accordingly.

PROVIDING QUALITY SERVICE
THROUGH SYSTEM CHANGES

System changes are expected if an organization is evolving and innovating as Associa has and continues to do, consistent with our company value of Innovation and Improvement. To be more specific about an otherwise vague and general term, "system changes" for the purposes of this discussion refers to changes in the following:

- **Business strategy.** This can include the pursuit of a new customer segment, the launch of a new product, or any other shift that would cause us to adjust our focus and therefore impact current customers.

- **Processes and Procedures.** Whenever we change how we execute tasks that affect customers, they will feel the impact. Even if the change is beneficial in the long run, managing short-term pain is crucial to retaining customers and providing them the five star service they deserve.

- **Technology.** Many of the tools Associa uses also must be fully adopted by our board members, and sometimes our homeowners, to be successful. Adjustments in this area, as with any other, may cause inconvenience to customers when they must change their own actions.

The impact on customers in each of these areas can be mitigated. Because no organization is perfect, however, some of the customer impact may be unavoidable because of the nature of the change or because mistakes may be made along the way. These realities result from the following challenges of providing quality service through system changes:

- **Change makes employees' jobs more difficult during the adjustment.** As the change is taking place, employees are putting time and energy into adapting through their roles and duties. Unless mitigated, the resulting stress could translate into a strain on serving our customers at our expected levels.

- **Providing customer service can take more time.** In times of change, fulfilling the needs of customers and correcting mistakes might be less efficient in the short term while the organization is trying to divide its time between maintaining operations and making a major adjustment.

A good learning example of a large-scale change in systems for Associa was the implementation of a centralized and automated accounts payable system to process all our client bills. We implemented this new technology in 2013 as a better means to safeguard client funds and to improve processing times and service. Today that system has achieved all that we envisioned and more, and our employees and clients see it as a beneficial and normal part of daily operations. Getting to this point, though, was a rocky road.

We expected the initial implementation to be painful, as it required employees and clients to conform to an entirely new way of doing things, using a digital process and abandoning their old habits of using paper invoices and live checks. To help our employees and clients through the change curve, it was critical we have a solid change management plan in place. The plan we carefully developed included communication, training, and assessment of impact.

While I'd love to say it was a seamless transition, that is far from the truth. This major change in process, procedure, and technology was fraught with challenge. We quickly learned that our carefully crafted plan did not address adequately the difficulty in changing human behavior, the true extent of ongoing training that would be required, and the steps necessary to recover from transitional issues with the technology. Never had we been as challenged to serve through change, and the quality of our service to our customers suffered as a result.

Thankfully, this implementation was done in phases, and as each new phase rolled out, our learnings from the previous phase made the next transition a little easier. We learned many valuable lessons from this initiative. We found that the keys to making successful large-scale change were to listen intently to our employees and clients, respond meaningfully to their feedback, and help them through the transition until they felt wholly comfortable. This experience and these lessons continue to inform our planning and strategy whenever we undertake large-scale initiatives as a company.

PROVIDING QUALITY SERVICE THROUGH ORGANIZATIONAL CHANGE

Although organizational change, much like system change, is a natural part of an organization's growth, it often is unexpected. When key personnel leave the organization, for example, timely decisions must be made about how to handle their job duties, and finding the best fit for the open position can place an additional strain on leaders, employees, and, eventually, customers. The challenges often extend beyond these concerns, however, and include the following:

- **Effect on relationships.** We would be remiss to overlook the human bonds we form in the workplace. When a leader leaves, or the organizational chart is redrawn, changes can affect our relationships at work.

- **Concerns of clients.** A shift in leadership could cause clients to wonder about the company's stability and the impact on customer service. This type of change also can cause uncertainty and raise a host of questions about the organization's direction.

- **Concerns of employees.** Along with possibly coping with a personal toll, employees might harbor worry and uncertainty about the future of their workplace, both in terms of mission and stability.

Providing the best customer service and maintaining high employee morale while meeting these challenges require managing the situation effectively by communicating proactively and reassuring stakeholders that service will remain uninterrupted during a change in leadership.

Since 1979 Associa has had many personnel and leadership changes, which is expected of any company as large and tenured as we are. As Associa has grown through the years, we've experienced some difficult challenges when key leaders have retired or moved on to other opportunities. These are much easier to handle when sufficient notice is given for planning purposes but much harder when departures are unexpected.

USING CHANGE MANAGEMENT TO HELP ENSURE CONSISTENT SERVICE

To address the challenges resultant from system or organizational change and deliver high levels of customer service throughout, we've found that change management techniques are essential. For Associa, the most successful approaches have included the following:

- **Redesigning processes.** When system or leadership shifts affect customers significantly, we must adapt to meet their needs and interests, including by redesigning processes appropriately.

- **Ensuring proper training.** Teaching employees how to deliver five star customer service in light of a change goes a long way toward ensuring that relationships with customers are maintained and enhanced, despite the discomfort they might be experiencing. Training can include instruction about the change itself and/or how to help customers deal with new systems and processes.

- **Executing thoughtful internal and external communication.** As part of planning for any change, it's crucial that well-rounded communication strategies are designed and implemented. These communications ease the transition for both employees and customers by giving them vital information for navigating the change and for maintaining relationships by being transparent, available, and accessible.

Serving customers well through times of change takes a great deal of forethought, time, and empathy. While we don't always get it right, calling on these resources to accomplish change well goes a long way toward maintaining a five star customer service experience while making improvements that will benefit all of our customers.

• • •

Anticipating the future needs of our clients and customers is a factor in the changes we make at Associa. Committed to serving through change, we listen carefully and adapt to feedback as we determine how, why, and when we must change our system, organization, or services. It isn't always easy, but we are determined to evolve positively and efficiently for the benefit of those we serve now and in decades to come.

SERVICE IN ACTION

Implementing change management best practices is especially important to mitigating the effects a shift in leadership can have on our employees and customers. In 2014, for example, one of the key leaders in one of our large branches retired unexpectedly. This individual was the original owner of the branch and joined Associa through acquisition. Our first step was to avoid overreacting to the departure because doing so could instill additional fear and confusion among employees and clients. Realizing that confidence and a well-considered plan of action are keys to making sound decisions based on reason and not on the emotions of the moment, we agreed that it was acceptable not to select a successor immediately.

Immediately upon learning about this leader's decision, we dispatched members of our executive team to visit the branch. They met with staff and reminded them that the company is strong because of our team, not one person. While we celebrated the retirement, our message helped instill confidence in the branch employees that they were still more than capable of serving our customers during this adjustment.

Associa prides itself in having succession planning, and in this case, there was a solid second-in-command at the ready. A transition plan is a major component of managing change, and having that plan, along with leadership presence on-site, reassured this branch's team and clients. Because they had been properly equipped for the change in leadership, both employees and clients were comfortable with the idea that it takes time to assess a situation and replace a good leader with another good leader. If there were not a solid successor, we would have supported the team and then found an appropriate replacement.

QUESTIONS TO CONSIDER

1. What is your current change management process?

2. What are your organization's strengths and weaknesses in managing change?

3. How can you use those insights to improve your customers' experience during change?

PART VI

OUR WAY

FORWARD

OUR WAY FORWARD

Customer service is not a department. It's a philosophy to be
embraced by everyone in an organization. Everyone plays
their part in contributing to the customer's experience.

—SHEP HYKEN,
Customer Service Expert

INTRODUCTION

To retain our leadership position in the community association management industry, we must constantly look ahead to identify, adapt
to, and even create the changes in the business and legislative envi-
ronments. Simultaneously, we must remain focused on the principles
and culture that enabled us to realize our mission on a global scale.
Associa's commitment to customer service involves every employee at
every level at every location, especially as we look for new and innovative ways to be service leaders in the future. This requires building a
team of people who devote themselves to exceeding the expectations
of our customers, regardless of the challenges they face.

Balancing our responsibilities as industry leaders and as service
providers will be essential as we strive to understand, meet, and predict the changing needs of our clients and customers. As we see new
trends in their behaviors and mindsets, we must adapt our service
model and implement operational initiatives that continue to meet

the standard we've set for five star customer service. This entails not only continually striving to exceed the expectations of our internal and external customers but also giving back to the communities beyond the associations we manage. Doing so is at the core of our daily operations and of our plans for the future.

The two chapters that compose Part VI describe how we measure our progress and how Associa hopes to continue to lead the way in service and products as we prepare for the changes we know will come in our industry and beyond.

CHAPTER 23

Measuring Our Momentum

What gets measured gets managed.

—PETER DRUCKER,
Management Consultant and Author

Our intent is to continue to create change within the field of community management, not simply to adapt to it or wait for others to create it. To do this, we must constantly measure our performance and our progress and use that information in our quest to innovate and to improve.

Associa is proud to be a learning organization. This means that we learn from our experiences—both successes and failures—and apply what we learn to get better every day. This could not be more important than in the area of measuring client satisfaction, which is why we regularly assess our service levels and work with them to resolve any gaps.

MEASURING OUR PROGRESS INFORMALLY

Managing community associations requires communication among the community management team, boards of directors, and homeowners. This ongoing process provides opportunities for instant assessments about a client's satisfaction. Areas that we discuss routinely with our clients include satisfaction with the maintenance of the property, the quality and accuracy of billing statements, and our responsiveness to requests from board members and homeowners. The way we handle these routine requests must be a high priority for our team if we are to retain our current clients and gain new ones.

Typically, as part of this check-in process, a branch leader will contact the board president and arrange a time and place to discuss the community and his or her satisfaction with our services in detail. The purpose of this meeting is simple: to ensure that we are offering the required support at the expected level of excellence. We are particularly interested in learning about the areas of our operation that are working well and about any that might need improvement. While sometimes we may want to assume a quiet client is a happy client, I learned long ago that this is not always the case.

During a scheduled conversation with one of our Nevada branch office's largest clients, for example, we received confirmation that our local service team was meeting expectations in most areas but also learned about an opportunity for improvement. Accordingly, we implemented our online invoice approval process, giving board members 24/7 online access to their association's financial information, including the ability to review and approve current invoices, review paid bills, and research expense details. Homeowners and board members who had a high level of understanding and expectations about our use of technology were thrilled, and so were we.

What's more, while discussing that significant and welcomed improved service, we learned about some opportunities to improve our website functionality. We had the exact solution board members were looking for and were able to arrange implementation quickly to meet their needs. They loved our quick response and also praised our local team's day-to-day efforts and the support provided by branch leadership to their homeowners and board.

MEASURING OUR PROGRESS FORMALLY

This ongoing informal process of collecting and responding to qualitative feedback is essential. We bolster it with our formal client survey process, which gives us quantitative results. Although we partner with an outside company for this purpose, we monitor the results frequently and invite our clients to contact us directly if they want to discuss their challenges or concerns with leaders from our home office.

While she was answering our formal survey, for example, the board treasurer of a garden-style townhouse community in the San Francisco Bay Area requested a personal follow-up from one of our senior leaders. She was a loyal customer of the local Associa branch but was troubled by some recent events that had occurred there. Their long-term community manager left suddenly at the beginning of the year, due to illness. Although the new manager assumed his duties enthusiastically, he was having trouble keeping up with projects and had arrived late to the last board meeting. The board member said she did not want to change management firms but was starting to consider her options.

We appreciated her candor and assured her that we would resolve the situation to her satisfaction. The local leadership team immediately created a plan to support the manager, monitor his performance, and keep the board informed along the way. The end result was positive. Our proactive request for feedback enabled us to restore the trust of this board member and the community—and keep a loyal client.

USING INDUSTRY MEASURES

In conjunction with our internal survey efforts, we track industry research so we can compare our internally collected data to data regarding the state of the industry, the satisfaction of boards and homeowners, and the perception of other management firms.

In fact, the Foundation for Community Association Research, the nonprofit arm of the Community Associations Institute, published a 2016 report titled *Americans Grade Their Associations, Board Members and Community Managers*. Its results indicate overwhelmingly that community residents find value in living in community associations. Some of the findings are listed below:

- 90 percent rated the experience as positive (64 percent) or neutral (26 percent).
- 83 percent said that their community managers provide value and support to residents and their associations.
- 88 percent of residents who had direct contact with their community managers say they had positive experiences.
- 90 percent confirm that association board members serve in the best interests of the community.

Our independent customer outreach and five star customer service efforts seek to improve those results, and all indications are that we are on the right track. Our success is validated by our impressive client retention rate, although our goal is to never lose a client.

COLLECTING AND RESPONDING TO FEEDBACK

To complement our informal client touch points and our client survey, we launched two additional feedback opportunities in 2016. Our Employee Advisory and Client Advisory Boards are two more vehicles through which we listen to, respond to, and learn from our employees, clients, and customers.

The Employee Advisory Board is made up of some of our best employees from all levels and from multiple locations. By listening to those who serve our clients and customers daily, we gain a better understanding of how to improve their experience and their service. We meet with this group monthly to discuss and listen to feedback about company strategies that impact our employees and clients.

Members are encouraged to raise relevant discussion topics. This is a great way to understand how employees feel and how they will respond to the things we do as a company to improve employee morale, which as mentioned earlier, is the key to our success at Associa. These discussions also are an excellent way to receive employee feedback about how they and their clients may react to changes in business processes, technology, or new products.

The Client Advisory Board consists of clients from each major market and customer segment. They help us improve our client experience by providing feedback about subjects such as how we can do a better job of helping them realize their visions for their communities and how we can enhance existing services and products or consider new ones that may meet their needs.

The goal with this group is to create meaningful client-focused dialogue about important community management and lifestyle matters. Collecting and responding to feedback from clients about what they think and what is important to them can be extremely illuminating. Sometimes their responses do not match our initial impressions, opinions, or expectations about how a strategy, product, or service would impact their client experience. This information enables us to reflect on and rethink our approach.

• • •

Being a learning organization requires us to be open to all kinds of feedback from employees and clients. We welcome these opportunities to listen to their voices and use the information gained in those discussions to get better every day. Together we are creating the future of our five star service and of Associa.

SERVICE IN ACTION

The following excerpt from a communication received by our office in Vancouver, British Columbia, is evidence that we have learned the importance of delivering five star service every day. A wonderful letter like this is an example of the qualitative measurements that are part of our innovation and improvement process:

Dear Management,

I'd like you to know how impressed I am with your manager. She is one of the most capable, efficient people I've dealt with in a while. I called in to ask a few questions about several units we own and she helped me immensely.

- *She didn't have to ask me anything over again because she listened the first time and understood exactly what I needed.*

- *She paced the information she provided me perfectly so I could write it down without pressure or confusion.*

- *She wrote my responses down so the second time I called in, she already had the notes on my units in front of her (wow).*

- *The second time I called, she was totally friendly and polite and just as efficient. For example, not showing annoyance that the customer forgot to do something on the first call.*

- *She is technically savvy and got me set up on the website very smoothly. I also received her confirmation email seconds after she said she'd send it.*

You don't find gems like her every day. I deal with so many people in my job, that when I get service this good it restores my faith in customer service and great hiring. Hats off to your manager and hats off to you for employing her!

QUESTIONS TO CONSIDER

1. How do you measure your progress in providing customer service?

2. How do you use the results of those measurements to improve?

3. How can you get more accurate or more frequent measurements of your service efforts?

CHAPTER 24

Continuing to Lead the Way

Let's go invent tomorrow instead of
worrying about what happened yesterday.

—STEVE JOBS,
Cofounder of Apple

Early on I saw that creating long-term success as a company meant differentiating ourselves from our competitors in both the way we thought about customer service and the way we approached delivering that service to our customers. It also meant we must commit dollars to growing the company while at the same time creating new methods and processes that were innovative for our industry. With that in mind, I have always welcomed the opportunity to share in creating the future of our business and of our industry, instead of simply reacting to changes brought about by others.

Associa may have started small, but we quickly grew into a widely dispersed and diverse group of management companies serving a variety of markets. To maintain this level of success today and in the future, we must be prepared for the changes we know will come to our industry and to the market in general. Customers today have the same expectations for every business with which they interact: They want the best service, and they want it now. The speed at which service and service recovery is demanded has increased greatly in the years since Associa's inception.

To keep up and to stay ahead of changes within and beyond our industry, we need to keep our focus on two main areas: investment in our people and investment in technology. At the same time we are preparing our employees to handle more complex customer interactions, we must research new and better ways of serving our clients through multiple channels, which should eliminate many basic transactions by allowing customers to self-serve.

We are blessed to attract and maintain a group of highly imaginative and dedicated professionals who are all instrumental in Associa's success. They work at all levels in the organization and offer feedback that helps us define the changing needs of our customers. Working together, we will identify ways to implement improvements and innovations in processes and delivery systems necessary to achieve the principles embodied in our Five Star Customer Service Model now and in the future.

Innovation is such a way of life at Associa that we are always thinking of and planning for what is next. We are a changing organization as much as we are a learning organization. In fact, every year we have multiple changes planned that compete for internal resources. I wish we could do them all, but that's not possible.

This is certain, however: At Associa we never will be satisfied merely to remain competitive and up to date. We intend always to be at the forefront of strengthening and improving our industry. Along the way we will learn from others, just as they will learn from us.

INVESTING IN OUR PEOPLE

Preparing for the future is the most critical challenge any organization faces. While it can be unpredictable, there are a few key activities that will ensure we are ready for whatever lies ahead. By focusing on the level of leadership we have within Associa and the extensive training and education our employees receive at every level, we will be prepared to meet any challenge confidently.

As our company has grown from five to thousands of employees in forty years, I have worked to ensure that every leader who joins our Associa family or is promoted through the ranks shares our vision for serving our clients and impacting our industry. This is no easy feat, and occasionally I have had to reevaluate a decision I made about a particular leader, but I know that the strength of leadership within the organization is our most important factor in preparing for the future.

As we have grown to become the largest community management firm, our focus on talent has become both more important and more difficult. It is well known that we trade talent with competitors, and vice versa. Given the unique characteristics of our business, it can be difficult to go outside of our industry to find those who will fit well in our environment. Nevertheless, that is what I have been doing slowly for several years, specifically at the executive level. My intent is to ensure that Associa has both the best experts in the industry and the best leaders from other industries to enrich us with new ideas and move us forward. This balance has increased and enhanced our capability, resulting in greater growth and new innovations within our company.

In addition to focusing on leadership, we must continue to stress the training and education of our community managers. We heavily emphasize the growth and development of employees at all levels, both because of the pipeline that we create for future leaders within our company and because of the greater service level we can provide for our customers.

Associa's commitment to training and developing our employees differentiates us from our competitors today and will be a critical success factor to our relationships with our clients and customers in the future. They expect us to act on their behalf and to have the most current information about the laws and policies that impact their communities. This is an unspoken expectation that is part of good service within our business now and always.

Through both the selection and development of our leaders and the growth and development of our employees, we will continue to lead as we prepare for the future. While I cannot predict with certainty what technological or cultural advancement will impact our industry, I am confident that if we have the best leaders and the best employees, we will not merely be prepared but will excel.

INVESTING IN TECHNOLOGY

Truly, we are focused on innovation in our company and in our industry, and technology plays a large role in it. As technology changes and presents greater opportunities to impact our industry and serve the needs of our clients, we respond appropriately.

This is especially true regarding how we deliver five star customer service. Responsiveness and instant gratification are becoming more and more important, and the best companies are striving to use technology to meet these ever-evolving expectations. At the time this book was written, for example, the taxi industry was being disrupted by Uber and other ride-sharing companies, and the cable industry by companies like Netflix streaming content. Associa must look for ways to best serve our clients by unlocking the power of our size and forecasting as accurately as possible the way our clients will want and need to be served for many years to come. Doing so will enable us to adapt as necessary to exceed their changing expectations.

The future of service technology is in balancing the client's need to self-serve with the traditional service model. Customers will expect both, but the number of those who prefer to visit physical office locations or make personal telephone calls is decreasing each year. People want the option to use their mobile devices to accomplish most of their basic service tasks. They want companies to engage with them via social media or text/instant message them to communicate. To keep up with the fast pace of this communication revolution, we must continue to innovate and use technology to facilitate providing better customer service.

SOCIAL MEDIA AS A SELF-SERVICE TOOL

We live in a time of instant communication. Email, text messaging, and social media channels allow people to connect regarding a variety of interests and issues. For service companies like Associa, technology affords us another outlet for addressing customer needs.

Despite the challenges and the reach of social media, Associa has the opportunity to identify and respond to customer issues that otherwise may have gone unanswered. Associa has made significant investments in developing our service recovery protocol for the social media platform. In the last several years we've engaged the entire company to help resolve issues posted online and have used negative reviews to generate positive, sustainable results. Our process is described on the next page.

With a standardized process, many of the questions our employees might normally have about resolving negative reviews are answered, allowing them to learn this aspect of customer service quickly.

Additionally, social media has given both Associa and our customers new ways to interact outside of reviews. We often receive questions via our social platforms and other online outlets that have nothing to do with complaints but are instead seeking information relevant to performing roles as board members and homeowners. Interacting with customers this way is more convenient not only for them but also for us. We reap the benefits of delivering an answer through social media because it saves us time and serves as a public demonstration of our approach to customer service.

What's more, social media has helped us build a community of involved board members and homeowners. While this doesn't directly affect customer service, it shows customers that we're willing to meet

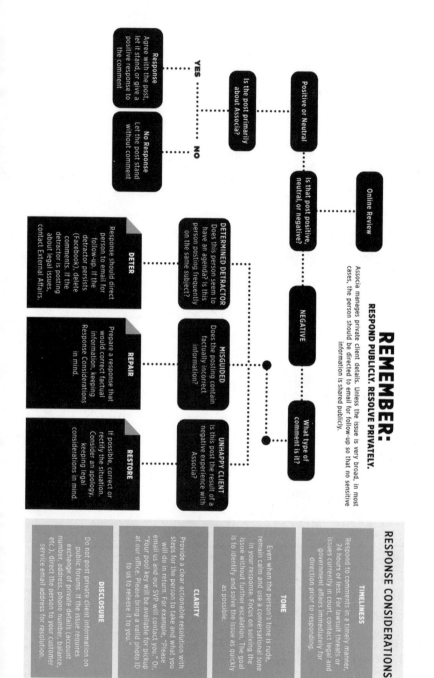

Associa Online Review Escalation Protocol

REMEMBER:
RESPOND PUBLICLY. RESOLVE PRIVATELY.

Associa manages private client details. Unless the issue is very broad, in most cases, the person should be directed to email for follow-up so that no sensitive information is shared publicly.

Online Review

Is that post positive, neutral, or negative?

Positive or Neutral

Is the post primarily about Associa?

YES · Response — Agree with the post, let it stand, or give a positive response to the comment

NO · No Response — Let the post stand without comment

NEGATIVE

What type of comment is it?

DETERMINED DETRACTOR — Does this person seem to have an agenda? Is this person posting frequently on the same subject?

DETER — Response should direct person to email for follow-up. If the detractor persists (Facebook), delete comments. If the detractor is posting about legal issues, contact External Affairs.

MISGUIDED — Does the posting contain factually incorrect information?

REPAIR — Prepare a response that would correct factual information, keeping Response Considerations in mind.

UNHAPPY CLIENT — Is this post the result of a negative experience with Associa?

RESTORE — If possible, correct or rectify the situation. Consider an apology, keeping legal considerations in mind.

RESPONSE CONSIDERATIONS

TIMELINESS
Respond to comments in a timely manner, 24 hours or less. For lawsuit threats or issues currently in court, contact legal and government affairs immediately for direction prior to responding.

TONE
Even when the person's tone is rude, remain calm and use a conversational tone in your response. Focus on solving the issue without further escalation. The goal is to identify and solve the issue as quickly as possible.

CLARITY
Provide a clear actionable resolution with steps for the person to take and what you will do in return. For example, "Please email us and our SVP will contact you." Or, "Your pool key will be available for pickup at our office. Please bring a valid photo ID to us to release it to you."

DISCLOSURE
Do not post private client information on public forums. If the issue requires exchange of private details (account number, address, phone number, balance, etc.), direct the person to your customer service email address for resolution.

them where they are and provide relevant content and information in the ways they want to receive it. Unlike many other self-service tools, social media as a whole is highly customizable for the customer, and we expect to see technology relevant to our customer service approach moving in that direction in the coming years.

ADAPTING TO TECHNOLOGY'S IMPACT ON CUSTOMER SERVICE

As technology allows customers to self-serve, live customer interactions are likely to become longer with greater complexity. Determining the appropriate level of investment between these two areas of technology and people is a difficult balance. Many of our homeowner issues can be handled quickly and easily, whether they involve a question about an account balance or how to make a payment. Others can be more difficult, including dealing with the emotion of receiving a violation letter, handling a dispute with a neighbor, and so on.

As a true service organization, our desire is to continue to serve our customers in the ways that they desire, not according to the easiest, cheapest, or most convenient or efficient way for Associa. While technology may be able to facilitate easy access to simple requests, we never can discount the value of human interaction. Rather than assume all our customers will prefer self-service, we must offer options and appropriate solutions for their issues.

An even more intriguing component of customer service technology is artificial intelligence (AI). It is part of many discussions about the future of technology, including in customer service. With big data and computing power, some computers already have passed the Turing test. This test, when passed, means a human cannot distinguish a machine or computer from another human. We are not far away from someone calling or interacting virtually with a machine and not even realizing it is not a person. This absolutely can disrupt the way we serve our customers, and we must be prepared for the impact of it and of other changes down the road.

We believe that an important part of minimizing the disruption to our customer service is to create positive technological disruption ourselves. As of this writing, Associa is preparing to launch the community management industry's first mobile app, and it will undoubtedly cause a shift in our customer service procedures. The tool allows board members, homeowners, and community managers to communicate with each other in one place and to benefit from a host of other functionalities relevant to customer service. Examples include the ability to make maintenance requests, pay assessments, and see the progress our community managers are making on projects.

While there are always unknowns with a shift of this magnitude, we know that the introduction of our app will streamline communication, reduce paperwork, securely store information, and help board members stay organized, which are all changes that can only improve our customers' experience. We also intend the app itself as an act of customer service because we want to adapt to the way many of our customers want to interact with us—not the other way around. The way that technology is changing customer service isn't a problem to fear and resist but, rather, is an opportunity to differentiate ourselves as a truly customer-focused organization.

• • •

Jean-Baptiste Alphonse Karr was right when he said, "The more things change, the more they remain the same." We have always succeeded in our business by changing and evolving, and we will continue to do so. Through our intense focus on strengthening our people and investing in the most up-to-date technology, we will continue to lead the industry for many years to come.

SERVICE IN ACTION

There are many examples of how our leaders have demonstrated courage and quick thinking to meet and exceed the expectations of our clients and customers. One of my favorite examples reflects not only the leadership of our employees but also their dedication to our clients:

> *When a three-alarm early-evening fire displaced residents of a twenty-one-unit, three-story building in a community we manage in a Chicago suburb, our Associa management team came through.*
>
> *Even though it was after hours, they hit the ground running, evacuating residents, locating their keys and other personal items, ensuring transportation, providing supplies, and securing the buildings.*
>
> *They worked through the night—some logging more than one hundred hours that week—to board broken windows, extract water, and even construct a temporary roof within forty-eight hours to protect the otherwise exposed building and its contents. They acted just in time: Another wave of storms hit the community the next day, ultimately dropping several inches of rain and spawning a tornado warning.*

The ability to plan for the immediate future is as important as planning for the long term, especially in precluding problems. This is a perfect example of the kind of outstanding leadership, selflessness, and responsiveness that personify our Five Star Customer Service Model. Our team's actions were impressive and inspiring, but no one wanted or expected credit. We are grateful to have them as part of the Associa family, and I'm confident they earned even deeper customer loyalty as a result of their hard work and dedication.

QUESTIONS TO CONSIDER

1. How do you see technology changing or possibly disrupting your industry? How are you responding to it?

2. How do leaders offer a competitive advantage to your company?

3. What are the knowledge and skills you and your coworkers must have to be prepared for the future?

CONCLUSION

The goal as a company is to have customer service
that is not just the best but legendary.

—SAM WALTON,
Founder of Walmart

Since we opened our doors as a small association management company in Dallas in 1979, Associa has evolved into the industry's leader. With hands-on management, twenty-four-hour customer service, and industry-leading experts who consistently deliver quality lifestyle planning, community governance, facilities management, accounting and financial services, and integrated services, we strengthen the communities we manage while preserving their property values. Above all, our extended Associa family strives always to offer the best products and services that are associated with legendary success.

Our focus on delivering five star customer service to our customers means we go above and beyond the ordinary not simply to meet their expectations but also to exceed them. Our continued success depends on our being proactive in meeting their changing needs and interests and in identifying innovative ways to keep them more than happy.

This aspiration starts first and foremost with our people. We search for the most qualified candidates from inside and outside the industry so that we build on established expertise and learn from new perspectives. As they become a part of the Associa family, our people learn how they are expected to treat and to serve one another so that these habits ultimately come through in how they serve our clients and customers. We also maintain continuing education as a high priority so that our leaders and employees stay abreast of the latest industry innovations in technology, best practices, and of course, customer service.

Success in serving our customers also requires our knowing who they are. We cannot assume that knowing their titles or roles is all the information we need to give them our best. Our people must understand the complexities of the roles both board members and homeowners play in community associations to meet their needs as well as our contractual obligations to them fully—from carrying out board directives to communicating effectively with homeowners.

This is all part of the service culture that we at Associa have created and on which we continue to build. We center every aspect of our culture—our values, pillars, goals, atmosphere, and attitudes—around service to each other and to our communities. It all starts with our mission, vision, values, and pillars and our employees' acceptance of them.

We keep our mission simple yet powerful: *Delivering unsurpassed management and lifestyle services to communities worldwide.* Immediately clear is that we cannot realize this statement without steadfast dedication to service, and to help our employees achieve that dedication, we live by our four pillars, namely, Employee Morale, Client Retention, Client Growth, and Profitability. The order of these pillars is critical. We believe that when employees are happy, they provide service that also keeps our clients happy to continue working with us. Because of their satisfaction, we are in a better position to utilize marketing and sales to grow. All of this culminates in profitability, which we can use to reinvest in Associa and our employees to further their morale. Along this continuum, we also strive to live in accordance with our values: Family Spirit, Loyalty, Integrity and Accountability, Innovation and Improvement, and of course, Customer Service.

All of this is the foundation for the heart of this book: Associa's Five Star Customer Service Model. The five stars, which are Demonstrate Care, Communicate Effectively, Exercise Leadership, Build Relationships, and Own the Resolution, are our aspiration for how we believe customer service should be carried out. Demonstrating care requires active listening, empathy, and total responsiveness. To communicate effectively, we must ensure that our customers receive our message and receive it in the way they expect it. Exercising leadership lies in our employees' ability to make tough decisions and do whatever it takes to serve the customer. Finally, by building relationships and owning the resolution, we strengthen the bonds we have with our clients and see to it that their needs are fully met—even beyond their own expectations.

These tenets are not limited to our external customers. They apply equally to our internal customers. This includes our employees, peers, and leaders, because at some time or another we all depend on each other, whether for information, to help serve a customer, or to earn a paycheck. By treating each other with five star customer service, our philosophy becomes more than merely buzzwords but, rather, a way of being authentic.

We live our service standards internally in several simple ways. Throughout every day and every interaction, we adhere to the Golden Rule, treating others the way we would like to be treated, as well as the Platinum rule, treating others the way they want to be treated. We also work to maintain friendly relationships, respond quickly, and show gratitude to each other. Especially important is that our leaders demonstrate these principles as well as live our company values to ensure that our clients, customers, and employees always come first.

With that precedent ingrained internally, we can apply five star customer service externally. This is the core of how we carry out our work, and it starts with demonstrating care. Beyond showing our value of Family Spirit through kindness and respect, we pay attention to the details, such as being positive, proactive, and personable. Second, our focus is on communicating effectively in not only what we say but also how we say it, the channels through which we say it, and our timeliness and thoughtfulness in responding. We display leadership by serving as expert advisors, build relationships with clients by building trust and friendship, and own the resolution by following through, no matter what.

Additionally, part of complete customer service is serving communities outside of the ones we manage, and we do that through our corporate citizenship programs: Associa Supports Kids, which provides enriching activities for children; Associa Green, which gives our communities support for environmental initiatives; and Associa Cares, which helps families whose homes have been affected by natural or man-made disaster. These efforts are an authentic expression of our commitment to community as a whole and are another avenue for our employees to live our values.

Because we are not perfect, a key component of excellent customer service is knowing how to handle shortcomings, which can take many forms. At times this requires managing the differing expectations of boards and homeowners because often an incident that appears to be a service mishap on the surface actually is a correct execution of our contract. In these situations, and in situations in which we truly made a mistake, it is critically important that we help the client or customer and make every effort to be of assistance. We do this through our customer service recovery process, which includes determining the issue that needs to be resolved, pinpointing the customer's ideal outcome, finding the source of the issue, and identifying the parties who can provide a resolution.

This process also extends to times when we experience a true customer service failure, which we acknowledge because no one expects organizations and individuals never to make mistakes. What is expected of us is to correct our mistakes with our customers immediately and completely. That is why we teach our employees to practice the popular acronym HEAT: Hear them out, Empathize, Acknowledge or apologize, and Take charge.

This preparation for service shortcomings helps us especially when Associa is undergoing change, which is a common occurrence due to our commitment to Innovation and Improvement as one of our values. During these times, internal customer service is most important to our employees so they can continue to provide stellar external customer service despite shifts in leadership, technology, and strategy.

Finally, throughout everything we do, we must measure our efforts both through the internal measures of client and employee feedback and through external measures such as comparing our collected data to industry standards. This gives us a multifaceted view of where we are excelling and where we can improve in our service efforts. Additionally, it informs our direction going forward and how we might prepare for the future. This includes investing in training and developing our people and in technology. We invest considerable thought, effort, and resources toward developing a variety of digital solutions to maximize efficiency and effectiveness for our communities, and we continue to do so by utilizing social media and launching our mobile app as tools for self-service. These combined efforts are how we plan to continue to lead the industry forward.

For us, customer service is more than a department or a value. It is the primary focus of every member of our Associa team, including our leaders, community managers, office personnel, and service technicians.

Our commitment to unsurpassed customer service means we are on duty at all times. We know we must always hold ourselves to the highest standards as members of Associa and on behalf of our clients. Recognizing that the easiest way to attract new clients is through our current clients, customers, and employees who recommend us, we work continually to merit their loyalty. The greatest compliment they can give us is to refer new customers and employees to be a part of our

Associa family. That is when we know we have gotten our Five Star Customer Service Model right.

Achieving this ideal is a building process. It does not happen overnight, and it is an aspirational standard that we pursue continually as part of who we are. That is our goal. That is our future. That is what it means to work in the common interest by truly embracing five star customer service.

ACKNOWLEDGMENTS

Writing this book has been a journey, not only to relay my thoughts about customer service in the community management industry, but also to ensure that at Associa we are living up to the standards we espouse. While still far from perfect, I believe as we conclude this writing process that we are closer to delivering five star service to every client, every day, every time than when we began.

I must start by thanking my wife, Helen, who has been by my side for many years in business and in life. She is as dedicated to my success and to the success of Associa as I am and always is my utmost encourager. Given that Family Spirit is our first company value, it is only appropriate that she and I lead first our family and then our larger Associa family together.

Additionally, many leaders at Associa contributed time and energy both to this book project and to ensuring we meet our service standards daily. No one played a larger role than Chelle O'Keefe, one of my most trusted advisors. Additionally, colleagues Matt Kraft, Debra Warren, Craig Koss, Andrew Fortin, Mike Packard, Cynthia Judson, and Helen Shacklett each played important roles. Writing a book is not a singular effort, and I am deeply grateful for each of them and for their support and advice.

I have built my career in the community management industry for many decades now and am humbled by the success our thousands of clients have helped us achieve. Without their trust and belief in our ability to serve them well, Associa would not exist. It has been my passion and my charge to wake up every day and continue to earn that trust by delivering on each of the principles of five star service.

May this book serve as our promise to our clients about what Associa will deliver to them and as a guide to our employees regarding how to serve, both internally to one another and externally to those who trust us with their business.

INDEX

A

accountability. *See also* owning the resolution
    as core value, 48
    Five Star Customer Service Model
        external customer service, 61–62
        internal customer service, 79–80
    retaining employees/team and, 110–11
accounting and financial services
    accounting portals, 153
    overview, 16
active listening, 144–45
AI (artificial intelligence), 233
Alessandra, Tony, 53
All I Really Need to Know I Learned in Kindergarten (Fulghum), 128
American Enterprise Institute, 187
Americans Grade Their Associations, Board Members and Community Managers (2016) report, 222
Amos, Wally, 57
apologizing
    building relationships and, 167
    correcting mistakes and, 200
    HEAT framework, 202, 241
artificial intelligence (AI), 233
ASK (Associa Supports Kids) program, 178–79, 240
Associa
    Client Advisory Board, 223
    community programs, 240
    continuing education programs, 13–14
    core services, 14–17
        accounting and financial services, 16
        community governance, 15
        facilities management, 15
        integrated services, 16–17
        lifestyle planning, 15
    culture of service, 35–63
        Five Star Customer Service Model, 53–63
        mission, 37–38
        overview, 35
        values, 45–52
    customer service relationship for community associations, 25

    determining responsibility in service recovery, 192–95
    Employee Advisory Board, 222–23
    employees/team, 13
    Five Star Customer Service Model, 239–40
    foundation of, 11–12
    giving back to community, 177–82
Associa Cares program, 180–81, 240
Associa Green program, 179–80, 240
Associa Supports Kids (ASK) program, 178–79, 240
association members (members)
    defined, 5
    services provided for, 24
associations. *See* community associations
Associa University (AU), 91–94
    evaluations, 94
    licensing and certification, 93
    overview, 91–93
    video teleconference system, 93
audience analysis (communication skills), 136–38
awards
    e3 recognition program, 114–15
    "Hard Hat" award, 106
    MVP award, 107

B

best practices (internal customer service), 69–73. *See* also Five Star Customer Service Model
    friendly attitude, 71
    Golden Rule, 70
    overview, 69–70
    Platinum Rule, 70–71
    responsiveness, 71–72
    showing gratitude, 72
board members. *See* clients
board packets (reports), 140
boards of directors
    community management's responsibility to, 29–30
    management's dual relationship with homeowners and, 31–32, 188
    meeting management, 154–55

services provided for, 22–23
body language, 98, 139

C

Carlzon, Jan, 113
change management
  communicating effectively, 211–12
  implementing automated accounts payable
    system, 209
  redesigning processes, 211
  service in action example, 212–13
  training programs, 211
Client Advisory Board, 223
Client Growth pillar, 41–42
Client Retention pillar, 40–41
clients
  boards of directors, 22–23, 29–30
  Client Growth pillar, 41–42
  Client Retention pillar, 40–41
  defined, 5
  meeting expectations of, 30–31
  overview, 21
  retaining, 59–60
  survey process, 221
  third-party customer service, 24–26
client survey process, 221
commitment
  communication and, 100–101
  to employee training, 229
  to internal customers, 84–85
In the Common Interest: Embracing the New
  American Community (Corona), 2–3
communication
  change management and, 211–12
  communication of feelings, 138–39
  employee communication channels, 99–100
  external customer service, 135–49
    audience analysis, 136–38
    establishing reasonable expectations, 145
    listening skills, 144–45
    managing conflict, 145–46
    nonverbal, 138–40
    overview, 135–36
    reports (board packets), 140
    responsiveness, 141–43
    self-service tools, 143–44
    service in action example, 148–49
    varied channels of, 146–47
    verbal, 138–39
    writing skills, 147–48
  Five Star Customer Service Model,
    56–57, 78

listening skills, 98–99, 144–45, 201–2
  loyalty and commitment, 100–101
  responsiveness, 71–72, 141–43, 173
  service in action example, 101–2
community associations. See also clients
  community governance, 15
  defined, 5
  giving back to community at large, 177–82
  treating as our own, 130–31
community managers
  defined, 5
  dual relationship with boards of directors
    and homeowners, 30–31, 188
  service in action examples
    core values, 51
    importance of good relationship with
      board of directors, 31–32
    pillars of culture of service, 43–44
competition
  e3 employee recognition program, 113–19
  industry, 37
conflict, managing, 145–46, 174–75
continuing education programs
  Associa University, 91–94
    evaluations, 94
    licensing and certification, 93
    overview, 90–93
    video teleconference system, 93
  change management, 211
  leadership, 109
  online learning programs, 91–92
  overview, 13–14
core services, 14–17
  accounting and financial services, 16
  community governance, 15
  facilities management, 15
  integrated services, 16–17
  lifestyle planning, 15
covenants, defined, 187
Covey, Stephen, 171
crises, leadership during, 155–56
culture of service
  Five Star Customer Service Model, 53–63
    accountability, 61–62
    building relationships, 59–60
    communicating effectively, 56–57
    demonstrating care, 55, 77, 125–34
    leadership, 57–59
    overview, 53–54
    service in action example, 62–63
  mission, 37–38
  overview, 4, 35

pillars, 38–44
    Client Growth, 41–42
    Client Retention, 40–41
    Employee Morale, 39–40
    overview, 38–39
    Profitability, 42–43
values, 45–52
    customer service, 47–48
    family spirit, 46–47
    innovation and improvement, 49–50
    integrity and accountability, 48
    loyalty, 49
    overview, 45–46
customers. *See also* internal customer service
    defined, 6, 22
    engaging with, 164–65
    expectations of, 56–57
    homeowners, 24
    meeting expectations of, 30–31
    overview, 21
    third-party customer service, 24–26
Customer Service core value, 47–48
customer service recovery. *See* service recovery

D

demonstrating care (Five Star Customer
    Service Model)
    external customer service, 55, 125–34
    internal customer service, 77
Drucker, Peter, 219

E

e3 employee recognition program, 113–19
    awards, 114–15
    expansion of, 117–18
    job aides, 115
    origin of, 113–14
    service guidelines, 116
    service in action example, 118
education programs
    Associa University, 91–94
        evaluations, 94
        licensing and certification, 93
        overview, 90–93
        video teleconference system, 93
    change management, 211
    leadership, 109
    online learning programs, 91–92
    overview, 13–14
Einstein, Albert, 177
Eisenhower, Dwight D., 39
email

maintaining positive tone, 127
out-of-office message, 142
Employee Advisory Board, 222–23
Employee Morale pillar, 39–40
    accountability, 110–11
    communication and, 78
    leadership, 108–9
    overview, 105–6
    recognition, 106–7
    tools and resources, 109–10
    work-life balance, 107–8
employees/team
    e3 recognition program
        awards, 114–15
        expansion of, 117–18
        job aides, 115
        origin of, 113–14
        service guidelines, 116
        service in action, 118
    education programs
        Associa University, 91–94
        change management, 211
        leadership, 109
        online learning programs, 91–92
        overview, 90–91
    employee communication channels, 99–100
    Employee Morale pillar, 39–40
    Family Spirit core value, 46–47
    feedback, 101–2
    investing in, 228–30
    performance reviews, 99
    preparing for service recovery, 201–2
    retaining
        accountability, 110–11
        leadership, 108–9
        overview, 105–6
        recognition, 106–7
        service in action, 111
        tools and resources, 109–10
        work-life balance, 107–8
    rewarding, 113–19
    selecting, 89–90
errors. *See* mistakes/errors
evaluations, 94
Every Client, Every Day, Every Time pro-
    gram. *See* e3 employee recognition program
external customer service
    building relationships, 159–70
        apologizing, 167
        engaging with customer, 164–65
        establishing realistic timelines, 166
        overview, 159

owning the resolution, 167
partnerships, 163–64
positive first impressions, 161–63
positive last impressions, 168–69
service in action example, 169–70
sharing experiences, 165–66
trust, 160–61
communication, 135–49
audience, 136–38
establishing reasonable expectations, 145
listening skills, 144–45
managing conflict, 145–46
nonverbal, 138–40
overview, 135–36
reports, 140
responsiveness, 141–43
self-service tools, 143–44
service in action example, 148–49
varied channels of, 146–47
verbal, 138–39
writing skills, 147–48
demonstrating care, 125–34
being positive point of contact, 126–28
being proactive, 131–33
Golden Rule, 128–30
Other People's Shoes Rule, 128–30
overview, 125–26
Platinum Rule, 128–30
service in action, 133–34
treating community as if it's our own,
130–31
Five Star Customer Service Model, 55,
125–34, 239–40
giving back to community, 177–82
Associa Cares program, 180–81
Associa Green program, 179–80
Associa Supports Kids program, 178–79
overview, 177–78
service in action example, 182
leadership, 151–58
during crises, 155–56
demonstrating, 153–54
innovation and improvement, 156–57
meeting management, 154–55
overview, 151–53
service in action example, 157
overview, 4, 123–24
owning the resolution, 171–76
accepting responsibility, 171–72
accountability, 172
integrity, 172
managing conflict, 174–75

responsiveness, 173
service in action example, 175
relationship of internal customer service to,
84–85

F
face-to-face communication, 99–100, 127
facilities management, 15
Family Spirit core value, 46–47
feedback
from employees/team, 101–2
measuring progress via, 222–23
performance reviews, 99
requesting, 56
firefighting mode, 132
first impressions, 161–63
Five Star Customer Service Model
accountability, 61–62
building relationships, 59–60
communication, 56–57
demonstrating care, 55
external customer service
accountability, 171–76
building relationships, 159–70
communication, 135–49
demonstrating care, 125–34
leadership, 151–58
internal customer service, 75–80, 239
accountability, 79–80
alignment with values, 76–77
building relationships, 79
communication, 78
demonstrating care, 77
leadership, 78
overview, 75–76
leadership, 57–59
overview, 53–54, 239–40
service in action example, 62–63
flexible work schedules, 108
Foundation for Community Association
Research, 222
foundation of Associa service model
changes in industry, 11–12
clients and customers, 21–27
boards of directors, 22–23, 29–30
homeowners, 24
meeting expectations, 30–31
overview, 21
third-party customer service, 24–26
continuing education programs, 13–14
core services, 14–17
accounting and financial services, 16

community governance, 15
facilities management, 15
integrated services, 16–17
lifestyle planning, 15
employees/team, 13
overview, 4, 9
scope of, 12
Fritz, Jerry, 37
Fulghum, Robert, 128
fundraising (Associa Cares program), 180–81

G

Gates, Bill, 199
Golden Rule
external customer service, 128–30
internal customer service, 70
gratitude, showing, 72, 111
Great Place to Work® Institute survey, 101–2
Greenleaf, Robert, 81
Gregoire, Jerry, 9

H

Half, Robert, 29
"Hard Hat" award, 106
HEAT problem-solving framework, 202, 241
homeowners. *See also* customers
defined, 5
services provided for, 24
homeowners association (HOA), 5
Hsieh, Tony, 135
Hyken, Shep, 35, 217

I

Iacocca, Lee, 97
industry measures, 221–22
Innovation and Improvement core value,
49–50, 156–57
Integrated Community Management, 16
integrated services
Integrated Community Management, 16
overview, 16–17
Professional Services, 16
Integrity and Accountability core value, 48, 172
internal customer service
best practices, 69–73
friendly attitude, 71
Golden Rule, 70
overview, 69–70
Platinum Rule, 70–71
responsiveness, 71–72
showing gratitude, 72
communicating effectively, 97–103

employee communication channels,
99–100
listening skills, 98–99
loyalty and commitment, 100–101
overview, 97–98
service in action example, 101–2
e3 recognition program, 113–19
educating employees/team, 90–94
Associa University, 91–94
overview, 90–91
Five Star Customer Service Model, 75–80,
239
accountability, 79–80
alignment with values, 76–77
building relationships, 79
communicating effectively, 78
demonstrating care, 77
leadership, 78
overview, 75–76
service in action example, 80
leadership model, 81–87
leading by example, 83–84
overview, 81–83
relationship to external customer service,
84–85
service in action example, 85–86
overview, 4, 67–68
retaining employees/team, 105–11
accountability, 110–11
leadership, 108–9
overview, 105–6
recognition, 106–7
service in action, 111
tools and resources, 109–10
work-life balance, 107–8
rewarding employees/team, 113–19
selecting employees/team, 89–90
service in action example, 73
inverted pyramid model, 82–83

J

job aides (e3 recognition program), 115
Jobs, Steve, 227

K

Karr, Jean-Baptiste Alphonse, 234

L

leadership, 151–58
characteristics of good leadership, 152
during crises, 155–56
demonstrating, 153–54

effect of internal leadership on customers, 84–85

Five Star Customer Service Model, 57–59, 78

innovation and improvement, 156–57

leading by example, 83–84

maintaining leadership position in industry, 227–36

meeting management, 154–55

overview, 81–83, 151–53

retaining employees/team and, 108–9

service in action example, 85–86, 157

training programs, 109

licensing and certification, 93

lifestyle planning (community), 15

Lindsay, Dean, 75

listening skills

active listening, 144–45

overview, 98–99

service recovery and, 201–2

loyalty

communication and, 100–101

as core value, 49

M

maintaining leadership position in industry, 227–36

measuring progress, 219–25

mission, 238

online review escalation protocol, 232

pillars, 38–43, 238–39

scope of, 12

succession planning, 213

managers. *See* community managers

Mcgannon, Donald H., 151

meeting management, 154–55

Mehrabian, Albert, 138–39

members. *See* homeowners

mission

building, 37–38

statement of, 238

mistakes/errors. *See also* shortcomings in service

correcting, 200–201

HEAT problem-solving framework, 202, 240–41

learning from, 202–3

Most VALUEable Player" (MVP) award, 107

N

Nasser, Kate, 11

National Association of Town Watch (NATW) National Night Out events, 179

Netflix, 230

nonverbal communication, 138–40

O

observation, during communication, 98

on-demand education courses, 92

online learning programs, 91–92

organizational changes

change management, 211–12

providing service during, 210–11

Other People's Shoes Rule, 128–30

out-of-office messages

email, 142

phone, 141–42

owning the resolution, 61–62. *See also* accountability

building relationships and, 167

external customer service, 171–76

accepting responsibility, 171–72

accountability, 172

integrity, 172

managing conflict, 174–75

responsiveness, 173

service in action example, 175

P

partnerships, building, 163–64

peer-to-peer recognition, 106

Penney, J. C., 159

performance review process, 110

pets, bothersome, 165–66

phone tag, 139

pillars of culture of service, 38–44, 238–39

Client Growth, 41–42

Client Retention, 40–41

Employee Morale, 39–40

overview, 38–39

Profitability, 42–43

service in action example, 43–44

planned unit development (PUD), 5

Platinum Rule

external customer service, 128–30

internal customer service, 70–71

Porter, Donald, 185

proactive approach (demonstrating care), 131–33

problem-solving. *See* shortcomings in service

professionalism

leadership and, 151–52

work environment and, 109–10

Professional Services, 16
Profitability pillar, 42–43
progress, measuring, 219–25, 241
    feedback, 222–23
    formally, 221
    industry measures, 221–22
    informally, 219–20
    service in action example, 224
PUD (planned unit development), 5
"pulse" surveys, 101

R
relationships, building
    external customer service, 159–70
        apologizing, 167
        engaging with customer, 164–65
        establishing realistic timelines, 166
        overview, 159
        owning the resolution, 167
        partnerships, 163–64
        positive first impressions, 161–63
        positive last impressions, 168–69
        service in action example, 169–70
        sharing experiences, 165–66
        trust, 160–61
    internal customer service, 79
        trust, 79
    overview, 59–60
reports (board packets), 140
respect. See also Five Star Customer Service
    Model
    building relationships and, 160, 165
    leadership and, 152
responsibility, accepting, 171–72
responsiveness (timely responses)
    external customer service, 141–43
    internal customer service, 71–72
    owning the resolution and, 173
Richards, Damon, 69
"ride-along" sessions (leaders), 83
Roosevelt, Eleanor, 67
Ruskin, John, 125

S
Sanders, Betsy, 1
Schneider, Benjamin, 84
Schultz, Howard, 45
self-service tools, 143–44, 231
service failures, 240–41. See also shortcomings
    in service
service guidelines (e3 employee recognition
    program), 116

service in action examples
    change management, 212–13
    commitment to service, 17–18
    communicating effectively, 101–2
    core values, 51
    cost savings through operational efficiencies,
        26–27
    e3 recognition program, 118
    external customer service
        building relationships, 169–70
        communication, 148–49
        demonstrating care, 133–34
        giving back to community, 182
        leadership, 157
        owning the resolution, 175
    Five Star Customer Service Model, 62–63
    internal customer service, 73, 80, 85–86
    maintaining leadership position in industry,
        235
    manager's role within community, 31–32
    pillars of culture of service, 43–44
    quality of service, 224
    service recovery, 195–97, 203–5
    showing gratitude, 111
service recovery
    assessing issue, 189
    correcting mistakes, 200–201
    defining customer's desired outcome, 189
    determining Associa's responsibility in,
        192–95
    identifying agents of resolution, 192
    learning from mistakes, 202–3
    overview, 187–89
    preparing employees/team for, 201–2
    service in action example, 195–97, 203–5
    uncovering source of problem, 190–92
shortcomings in service
    change management, 211–12
        communicating effectively, 211–12
        redesigning processes, 211
        service in action example, 212–13
        training programs, 211
    during organizational changes, 210–11
    overview, 4, 185–86
    service recovery
        assessing issue, 189
        correcting mistakes, 200–201
        defining customer's desired outcome, 189
        determining Associa's responsibility in,
            192–95
        identifying agents of resolution, 192
        learning from mistakes, 202–3

overview, 187–89
> preparing employees/team for, 201–2
> service in action example, 195–97, 203–5
> uncovering source of problem, 190–92
> during system changes, 207–10
Sinek, Simon, 89, 105
social media, 143, 231–33
Spector, Robert, 123
Sta. Ana, Myron S., 187
strata managers. *See* community managers
stratas, defined, 5
succession planning, 213
success, maintaining, 227–36
> impact of technology on customer service, 233–34
> investing in employees/team, 228–30
> investing in technology, 230–31
> overview, 227–28
> service in action example, 235
> social media and, 231–33
system changes
> business strategy, 208
> change management, 211–12
> defined, 208
> mitigating impact on customers, 208–10
> process and procedures, 208
> providing service during, 207–10
> technology, 208

T
technology
> impact on customer service, 233–34
> investing in, 230–31
> social media, 143, 231–33
telephone conversations, maintaining positive tone, 127
thank-you notes, writing, 72, 107
third-party customer service, 24–26
timely responses. *See* responsiveness
tone of voice (communication), 139
tools and resources
> managing conflict, 146

> for retaining employees/team, 109–10
> self-service tools, 143–44, 231
training programs
> Associa University, 91–94
> > evaluations, 94
> > licensing and certification, 93
> > overview, 90–93
> > video teleconference system, 93
> change management and, 211
> leadership, 109
> online learning programs, 91–92
> overview, 13–14
troubleshooting. *See* shortcomings in service
trust, building relationships and, 79, 160–61, 166
Turing test, 233

U
Uber, 230
under promise/over deliver practice, 166–67
units, defined, 5

V
values
> aligning internal customer service with, 76–77
> Customer Service core value, 47–48
> Family Spirit core value, 46–47
> Innovation and Improvement core value, 49–50
> Integrity and Accountability core value, 48
> Loyalty core value, 49
> overview, 45–46
verbal communication, 138–39
video teleconference (VTC) system, 93

W
Walton, Sam, 237
Welch, Jack, 207
work-life balance, 107–8
writing skills (written communication skills), 147–48

ABOUT THE AUTHOR

JOHN CARONA is the founder and CEO of Associa, the industry's largest community management company. His vast experience and industry expertise encompass all aspects of residential real estate, including the development, leasing, management, and maintenance of single- and multi-family communities. For forty years, Associa has been an industry-leading innovator that has provided solutions designed to help communities thrive and achieve their vision. Under Mr. Carona's leadership, Associa achieved the Best Place to Work certification from Great Place to Work® and was named one of Dallas/Fort Worth's Best and Brightest Companies to Work For®.

A dedicated public servant, Carona served five terms in the Texas Senate and three in the Texas House of Representatives. He has been honored for his continued dedication to important issues, including public education, criminal justice, and economic development. His many honors include being named "Champion of Free Enterprise," "Crime Fighter of the Year," and "Most Valuable Player—Texas Senate" as well as one of Texas's "Ten Best Legislators."

Carona has an unmatched business sense and leadership ability that allows him to constantly evolve and revolutionize the ever-changing community management business. While running a growing global business; contributing to several charitable organizations, operating his own nonprofit charity, Associa Cares, and authoring several books, he remains family-focused. Born and reared in Texas, Carona graduated from The University of Texas at Austin and resides in Dallas with his wife, Helen. He is the loving father of five children and has eight grandchildren. An avid art collector, he enjoys traveling with his family, ranching, and hunting.